MW00904214

Building MATH FLUENCY

Grade 2

Consultant: Eleanor Falk Young
Editorial Development: Joy Evans
Jo Ellen Moore
Copy Editing: Carrie Gwynne
Art Direction: Cheryl Puckett
Cover Design: Liliana Potigian
Illustration: Jo Larsen
Design/Production: Arynne Elfenbein
Marcia Smith

EMC 3034

Evan-Moor
EDUCATIONAL PUBLISHERS®
Helping Children Learn since 1979

Congratulations on your purchase of some of the finest teaching materials in the world.

Correlated to State Standards

Photocopying the pages in this book is permitted for single-classroom use only. Making photocopies for additional classes or schools is prohibited.

For information about other Evan-Moor products, call 1-800-777-4362, fax 1-800-777-4332, or visit our Web site, www.evan-moor.com. Entire contents © 2008 EVAN-MOOR CORP. 18 Lower Ragsdale Drive, Monterey, CA 93940-5746. Printed in USA.

Visit *teaching-standards.com* to view a correlation of this book's activities to your state's standards. This is a free service.

Contents

Addition Tests

Subtraction Tests

Student Practice Flashcards

Answer Key

Transparencies

What's in This Book?

Mathematics standards frequently contain terminology such as "numerical fluency," "computational accuracy," and "automaticity." These terms recognize that the ability to compute quickly and accurately aids in higher-level mathematics and problem solving.

The goal of *Building Math Fluency* is to provide students with tools for thinking about computation in logical, strategic ways. Mastery of math facts is facilitated by understanding number relationships. Mastery is further enhanced with sufficient practice.

Strategy Practice

There is a section of strategy practice for each operation presented in this book. These practice pages can be done with students in a whole class or in small groups. Students benefit when teachers and peers model the use of the strategies and verbalize solution strategies aloud.

Charts of the strategies are presented both as reproducibles and as transparencies at the back of this book.

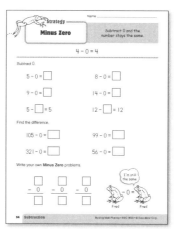

Practice pages feature a strategy box and problems to solve using that strategy.

Test Your Skills

The *Test Your Skills* pages provide concentrated fact practice. These pages can be used in a number of ways, as described on page 77. A feature of *Test Your Skills* is the opportunity for students to evaluate their own performance.

Facts Flashcards

Reproducible flashcards for the operations covered in this book are provided. The teacher resource page at the beginning of the section gives suggestions for using the cards to enhance students' mastery of number facts.

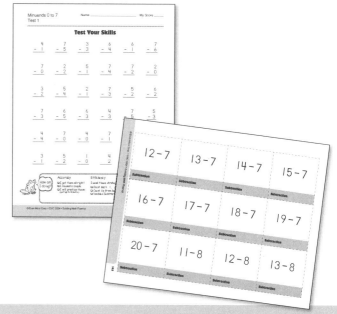

Glossary of Mathematics Terms

Addends The numbers in an addition problem.

$$3 + 4 = 7 \leftarrow \text{sum}$$
$$\uparrow \quad \uparrow$$
$$\text{addend}$$

Commutative Property of Addition Numbers can be added in any order without changing the sum.

$$3 + 4 = 7 \qquad 4 + 3 = 7$$

Difference The result of subtracting two numbers.

$$16 - 7 = 9$$
$$\uparrow$$
$$\text{difference}$$

Digit Any of the symbols 0, 1, 2, 3, 4, 5, 6, 7, 8, 9 used to write a number.

Fact Family A group of related facts, either addition or subtraction.

$$8 + 4 = 12 \qquad 4 + 8 = 12 \qquad 12 - 4 = 8 \qquad 12 - 8 = 4$$

Identity Property of Addition When 0 is added to a number, it does not change the total.

Minuend The number being subtracted from.

$$16 - 7 = 9$$
$$\uparrow$$
$$\text{minuend}$$

Place Value The value of a digit as determined by its position in the ones place, tens place, and so forth. Each position is ten times of the place to its right and one-tenth of the place to its left.

Subtrahend The number being subtracted.

$$16 - 7 = 9$$
$$\uparrow$$
$$\text{subtrahend}$$

Sum The result of joining quantities; the total.

$$3 + 4 = 7$$
$$\uparrow$$
$$\text{sum}$$

Teaching Addition Strategies

Pages 8–51 present practice with addition strategies that promote computational fluency and fact mastery.

Plus Zero means add 0 to any number and the number stays the same.

$$3 + 0 = 3$$

Count Up is an efficient strategy when adding a small number (1, 2, or 3) to a larger quantity. Students start with the larger addend and count up the smaller addend to find the total.

Turn Around means that the order of the addends does not change the total.

$$4 + 1 = 5 \quad \text{and} \quad 1 + 4 = 5$$

Doubles are facts in which an addend is added to itself. Students often discover that Doubles are always even numbers. When students have learned the Doubles facts, they have an "anchor" from which to compute many other facts.

$1 + 1 = 2$	$3 + 3 = 6$	$5 + 5 = 10$	$7 + 7 = 14$	$9 + 9 = 18$
$2 + 2 = 4$	$4 + 4 = 8$	$6 + 6 = 12$	$8 + 8 = 16$	$10 + 10 = 20$

Doubles Plus One means double the addend and add one more.

Doubles Facts	Doubles Plus One Facts
If you know $6 + 6 = 12 \longrightarrow$	then $6 + 7$ is just $6 + 6 + 1 = 13$
If you know $8 + 8 = 16 \longrightarrow$	then $8 + 9$ is just $8 + 8 + 1 = 17$

Tens Partners are number pairs that make 10.

$0 + 10 = 10$	$2 + 8 = 10$	$4 + 6 = 10$
$1 + 9 = 10$	$3 + 7 = 10$	$5 + 5 = 10$

Plus Ten means when 10 is added to a number, the tens-place digit increases by one, while the ones-place digit stays the same.

$$44 + 10 = 54$$

Plus Nine is based on the fact that 9 is one away from 10. Two common approaches are:

See 9. Think 10.	See 9 Make 10.
See $6 + 9$. Think $6 + 10 - 1$.	Turn $6 + 9$ into $5 + 10$.
See $14 + 9$. Think $14 + 10 - 1$.	Turn $14 + 9$ into $13 + 10$.

Building Math Fluency • EMC 3034 • © Evan-Moor Corp.

Addition Strategies

Plus Zero	Add 0 to a number and the number stays the same. $3 + 0 = 3$
Count Up $+1, +2, +3$	Count up when adding on small numbers, such as 1, 2, or 3.
Turn Around	Add numbers in any order and the total stays the same. $3 + 1 = 4 \qquad 1 + 3 = 4$
Doubles	Add the number to itself and that number doubles. $2 + 2 = 4$
Doubles Plus One	Double the number and add one more. $2 + 3 = 2 + 2 + 1$
Tens Partners	There are six sets of number pairs that make 10: $10 + 0 \qquad 9 + 1 \qquad 8 + 2$ $7 + 3 \qquad 6 + 4 \qquad 5 + 5$
Plus Ten	When 10 is added to a number, the tens-place digit increases by one. $12 + 10 = 22$
Plus Nine See 9. Think 10. See 9. Make 10.	To add 9 to a number, add 10 instead and jump back one. See $6 + 9$ Think $6 + 10 - 1$ **OR** To add 9 to a number, make the 9 a 10 by reducing the other addend by one. See $9 + 4$ Make $10 + 3$

Strategy

Plus Zero

Add 0 to a number and the number stays the same.

$$3 + 0 = 3$$

Add 0.

$7 + 0 =$ _____ $8 + 0 =$ _____

$0 + 9 =$ _____ $4 + 0 =$ _____

$5 + 0 =$ _____ $0 + 12 =$ _____

Add 0 to large numbers.

$100 + 0 =$ _____ $99 + 0 =$ _____

$0 + 232 =$ _____ $487 + 0 =$ _____

Write your own **Plus Zero** problems.

_____ $+ 0 =$ _____

_____ $+ 0 =$ _____

$0 +$ _____ $=$ _____

I am the same!

$+ 0 =$

Fred   Fred

Strategy
Count Up
+1, +2, +3

Count Up when adding on small numbers, such as 1, 2, or 3.

To solve $7 + 2$, start at 7. Circle 7.
Count up 2 hops. Underline the answer.

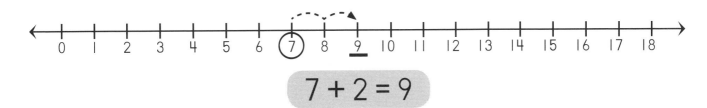

$$7 + 2 = 9$$

Add. Use the **Count Up** strategy.
Show your hops on the number line.

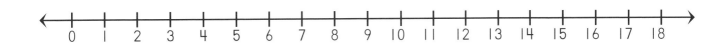

$$6 + 1 = \underline{\qquad}$$

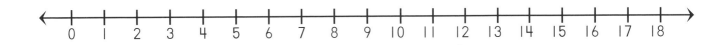

$$4 + 2 = \underline{\qquad}$$

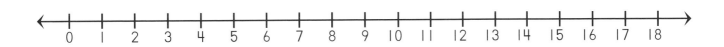

$$5 + 3 = \underline{\qquad}$$

Name _____

Strategy
Count Up
+1, +2, +3

Count Up to add a small number to a larger number.

Find the sums. Use the number line.

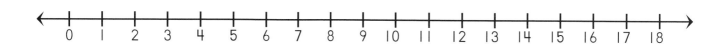

4 + 1 = _____   8 + 2 = _____   13 + 1 = _____

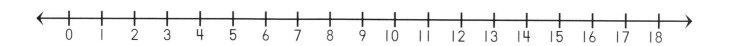

1 + 3 = _____   7 + 2 = _____   14 + 3 = _____

Add. Use the number line.

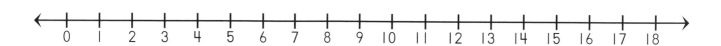

17 + 1 = _____   6 + 3 = _____   5 + 3 = _____

9 + 3 = _____   13 + 1 = _____   9 + 2 = _____

11 + 2 = _____   10 + 3 = _____   8 + 3 = _____

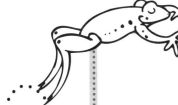

Strategy
Count Up
+1, +2, +3

Count Up to add a small number
to a larger number.

Solve the problems. Use the number line.

$19 + 1 =$ _____ $13 + 2 =$ _____

$16 + 1 =$ _____ $8 + 3 =$ _____

$19 + 2 =$ _____ $14 + 2 =$ _____

$$
\begin{array}{r} 18 \\ +\ 1 \\ \hline \end{array}
\qquad
\begin{array}{r} 5 \\ +\ 3 \\ \hline \end{array}
\qquad
\begin{array}{r} 17 \\ +\ 2 \\ \hline \end{array}
$$

$$
\begin{array}{r} 9 \\ +\ 3 \\ \hline \end{array}
\qquad
\begin{array}{r} 12 \\ +\ 2 \\ \hline \end{array}
\qquad
\begin{array}{r} 18 \\ +\ 3 \\ \hline \end{array}
$$

Write your own **Count Up** problems.

_____ + 1 = _____   _____ + 2 = _____

22
21
20
19
18
17
16
15
14
13
12
11
10
9
8
7
6
5
4
3
2
1
0

Strategy
Count Up
+1, +2, +3

Count Up to add a small number to a larger number.

Count how many jumps you need to get to the answer.

$6 + \boxed{} = 7$ $9 + \boxed{} = 11$

$3 + \boxed{} = 6$ $15 + \boxed{} = 16$

$12 + \boxed{} = 14$ $7 + \boxed{} = 10$

$$\begin{array}{r} 4 \\ + \boxed{} \\ \hline 7 \end{array}$$ $$\begin{array}{r} 10 \\ + \boxed{} \\ \hline 12 \end{array}$$ $$\begin{array}{r} 6 \\ + \boxed{} \\ \hline 9 \end{array}$$

$$\begin{array}{r} 15 \\ + \boxed{} \\ \hline 17 \end{array}$$ $$\begin{array}{r} 7 \\ + \boxed{} \\ \hline 8 \end{array}$$ $$\begin{array}{r} 13 \\ + \boxed{} \\ \hline 16 \end{array}$$

Number line: 17, 16, 15, 14, 13, 12, 11, 10, 9, 8, 7, 6, 5, 4, 3, 2, 1, 0

Strategy
Count Up
+1, +2, +3

Count Up to add a small number to a larger number.

Use the number line to solve the problems.

$5 + \boxed{} = 7$ $6 + \boxed{} = 8$

$8 + \boxed{} = 9$ $7 + 3 = \boxed{}$

$12 + 3 = \boxed{}$ $14 + \boxed{} = 17$

$$\begin{array}{r} 11 \\ + \boxed{} \\ \hline 13 \end{array}$$
$$\begin{array}{r} 5 \\ + 3 \\ \hline \boxed{} \end{array}$$
$$\begin{array}{r} 16 \\ + \boxed{} \\ \hline 17 \end{array}$$

Write your own **Count Up** problems.

$\boxed{} + 1 = \boxed{}$

$\boxed{} + 2 = \boxed{}$

$\boxed{} + 3 = \boxed{}$

$$\begin{array}{l} 17 \\ 16 \\ 15 \\ 14 \\ 13 \\ 12 \\ 11 \\ 10 \\ 9 \\ 8 \\ 7 \\ 6 \\ 5 \\ 4 \\ 3 \\ 2 \\ 1 \\ 0 \end{array}$$

Strategy

Count Up

+1, +2, +3

Count Up to add a small number to a larger number.

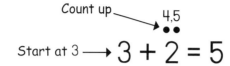

Count up → 4,5
• •

Start at 3 → 3 + 2 = 5

Start with the greater addend.
Draw dots as you **Count Up**.

5,6,7
• • •
4 + 3 = _7_

7,8
• •
6 + 2 = _____

7 + 2 = _____

8 + 3 = _____

10 + 3 = _____

5 + 3 = _____

12 + 2 = _____

17 + 3 = _____

11 + 3 = _____

16 + 2 = _____

19 + 3 = _____

28 + 3 = _____

79 + 1 = _____

91 + 2 = _____

Strategy
Count Up
+1, +2, +3

Count Up to add a small number to a larger number.

Circle the greater number.
Draw dots and **Count Up** from the largest addend.

7,8,9

$\textcircled{6} + 3 =$ _____ 9

6

$1 + \textcircled{5} =$ _____ 6

$10 + 2 =$ _____

$3 + 8 =$ _____

$16 + 3 =$ _____

$2 + 11 =$ _____

$14 + 2 =$ _____

$1 + 15 =$ _____

$3 + 9 =$ _____

$3 + 13 =$ _____

$7 + 3 =$ _____

$18 + 1 =$ _____

$9 + 2 =$ _____

$3 + 15 =$ _____

Try these.

$29 + 3 =$ _____

$38 + 3 =$ _____

Strategy
Count Up
+1, +2, +3

Count Up to add a small number to a larger number.

Solve the problems.

$$15 + 2$$

$$17 + 3$$

$$21 + 2 =$$

$$18 + 3 =$$

$$19 + 2$$

$$16 + 2$$

$$3 + 10 =$$

$$3 + 11 =$$

$$15 + 3$$

Think about how you solved the problems. Mark **yes** or **no**.

Did you:		yes	no
draw dots to count up?	$19 + \overset{\bullet\bullet}{2}$	☐	☐
count up from the larger number?	$\boxed{19} + 2$	☐	☐
use a number line?	←—⊢——⊢——⊢——⊢—→ 19 20 21 22	☐	☐

Strategy

Turn Around

Add numbers in any order and the total stays the same.

When you learn one addition fact, you really learn two.

_____ + _____ = _____   turn around   _____ + _____ = _____

_____ + _____ = _____   turn around   _____ + _____ = _____

_____ + _____ = _____   turn around   _____ + _____ = _____

Write the **Turn Around** fact.

$1 + 5 = \underline{} + \underline{}$

$7 + 4 = \underline{} + \underline{}$

$13 + 5 = \underline{} + \underline{}$

$99 + 1 = \underline{} + \underline{}$

$4 + 3 = \underline{} + \underline{}$

$10 + 2 = \underline{} + \underline{}$

$2 + 9 = \underline{} + \underline{}$

$100 + 3 = \underline{} + \underline{}$

Doubles

Name _____

Add the number to itself and
that number doubles.

Solve the **Doubles** facts.

_3_ + _3_ = _6_

_____ + _____ = _____

_____ + _____ = _____

_____ + _____ = _____

_____ + _____ = _____

_____ + _____ = _____

_____ + _____ = _____

Building Math Fluency • EMC 3034 • © Evan-Moor Corp.

Strategy

Doubles

Add the number to itself and that number doubles.

Match the picture with the **Doubles** fact.

- 3 + 3 = _____

- 8 + 8 = _____

- 6 + 6 = _____

- 5 + 5 = _____

- 4 + 4 = _____

Double 7. Make 7 tally marks on the first line. Then solve the problem.

||||| || + _____   7 + 7 = _____

Strategy

Doubles

Add the number to itself and that number doubles.

Draw dots to complete the double dominoes.
Write the equations.

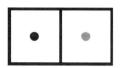

$1 + 1 = \underline{2}$

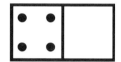

____ + ____ = ____

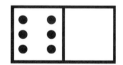

____ + ____ = ____

$3 + 3 = \underline{\hspace{1cm}}$

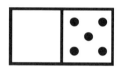

____ + ____ = ____

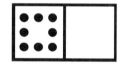

____ + ____ = ____

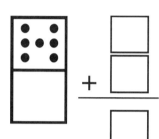

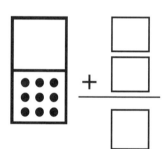

Draw dots to make double dominoes. Complete the equations.

____ + ____ = 10

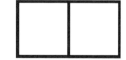

____ + ____ = 16

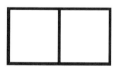

____ + ____ = 8

____ + ____ = 14

Building Math Fluency • EMC 3034 • © Evan-Moor Corp.

Strategy

Doubles

Add the number to itself and that number doubles.

Make tally marks to help you find the sum. Complete the chart.

Doubles Fact	Tally Marks	Sum
1 + 1	┆ + ┆	2
2 + 2		
3 + 3		
4 + 4		
5 + 5		
6 + 6	卌 ┆ + 卌 ┆	
7 + 7		
8 + 8		
9 + 9		
10 + 10		
11 + 11		
12 + 12		
13 + 13		

Describe the pattern in your sums. _____

Strategy

Doubles Plus One

Double the number and
add one more.

Double the number.   Add one more.

```
  4  ○○○○              4  ○○○○
+ 4  ○○○○           + 5  ○○○○●
―――                  ―――
  8                    9
```

Solve the **Doubles** fact. Then solve the **Doubles Plus One** fact.

Doubles	Doubles + 1

```
  5  ○○○○○                    5  ○○○○○
+ 5  ○○○○○                 + 6  ○○○○○●
―――                         ―――
```

```
  6  ○○○○○○                   6  ○○○○○○
+ 6  ○○○○○○                + 7  ○○○○○○●
―――                         ―――
```

```
  7  ○○○○○○○                  7  ○○○○○○○
+ 7  ○○○○○○○               + 8  ○○○○○○○●
―――                         ―――
```

```
  8  ○○○○○○○○                 8  ○○○○○○○○
+ 8  ○○○○○○○○              + 9  ○○○○○○○○●
―――                         ―――
```

Name _____

Strategy

Doubles Plus One

Double the number and
add one more.

Doubles Fact
Double the number.

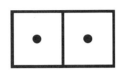

$| + | = 2$

Doubles Plus One Fact
Add one more dot and solve.

$| + 2 = \underline{3}$

Write the **Doubles** equation. Then write the **Doubles Plus One** equation.

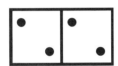

____ + ____ = ____

____ + ____ = ____

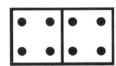

____ + ____ = ____

____ + ____ = ____

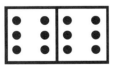

____ + ____ = ____

____ + ____ = ____

Strategy

Doubles Plus One

Double the number and
add one more.

Complete the number equations.

$3 + 3 =$ _6_   so $3 + 4 =$ _____

$5 + 5 =$ _____   so $5 + 6 =$ _____

$6 + 6 =$ _____   so $6 + 7 =$ _____

$8 + 8 =$ _____   so $8 + 9 =$ _____

$7 + 7 =$ _____   so $7 + 8 =$ _____

$9 + 9 =$ _____   so $9 + 10 =$ _____

Solve these.

$10 + 10 =$ _____   so $10 + 11 =$ _____

$20 + 20 =$ _____   so $20 + 21 =$ _____

$100 + 100 =$ _____   so $100 + 101 =$ _____

       Building Math Fluency • EMC 3034 • © Evan-Moor Corp.

Strategy

Doubles Plus One

Double the number and
add one more.

Solve and match.
Each **Doubles** fact has two **Doubles Plus One** facts.

Doubles Facts

3 + 3 = _____

4 + 4 = _____

5 + 5 = _____

6 + 6 = _____

7 + 7 = _____

8 + 8 = _____

Doubles + 1 Facts

5 + 6 = _____
6 + 5 = _____

3 + 4 = _____
4 + 3 = _____

4 + 5 = _____
5 + 4 = _____

6 + 7 = _____
7 + 6 = _____

8 + 9 = _____
9 + 8 = _____

7 + 8 = _____
8 + 7 = _____

Strategy

Tens Partners

Number pairs that make 10 are called **Tens Partners**.

Color the boxes to show **Tens Partners**.
Use blue for the first addend and orange for the second addend.

$9 + 1 = 10$

blue	blue	blue	blue	blue	blue	blue	blue	blue	orange

$8 + 2 = 10$

blue	blue	blue	blue	blue	blue	blue	blue	orange	orange

$7 + 3 = 10$

$6 + 4 = 10$

$5 + 5 = 10$

$4 + 6 = 10$

$3 + 7 = 10$

$2 + 8 = 10$

$1 + 9 = 10$

Strategy

Tens Partners

Number pairs that make 10 are called **Tens Partners**.

Color the row to show **Tens Partners**.
Use blue for the first addend and orange for the second addend.
Then record the number model to complete each row.

Number model

										Number model
blue	orange	orange	orange	orange	orange	orange	orange	orange	orange	1 + 9
blue	blue									2 + 8
									10 + 0

This is often called the "tens staircase."

Tens Partners

Number pairs that make 10 are called **Tens Partners**.

Count the dark and light circles in each ten frame.
Record the combinations of 10.

_____ + _____ = 10
  ●   ○

_____ + _____ = 10
  ●   ○

_____ + _____ = _____
  ●   ○

_____ + _____ = _____
  ●   ○

_____ + _____ = _____
  ●   ○

_____ + _____ = _____
  ●   ○

Complete the **Turn Around** facts.

$8 + 2 = 10$ and $2 + 8 = 10$ $6 + 4 = 10$ and _____

$1 + 9 = 10$ and _____ $3 + 7 = 10$ and _____

Strategy

Tens Partners

Number pairs that make 10 are called **Tens Partners**.

Solve.

$9 + \boxed{} = 10$ $7 + 3 = \boxed{}$ $5 + \boxed{} = 10$

$$\begin{array}{r} 8 \\ + \boxed{} \\ \hline 10 \end{array}$$ $$\begin{array}{r} 6 \\ + \boxed{} \\ \hline 10 \end{array}$$ $$\begin{array}{r} 1 \\ + \boxed{} \\ \hline 10 \end{array}$$ $$\begin{array}{r} 4 \\ + \boxed{} \\ \hline 10 \end{array}$$

Circle the **Tens Partners**.

8 and 2   9 and 3   4 and 5

7 and 2   1 and 9   10 and 0

6 and 4   3 and 8   7 and 3

Write the number pairs that make 10.

0 + 10	10 + 0	1 + 9	9 + 1		

Do you know the number pairs that make 10?

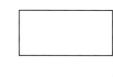

Strategy

Plus Ten

When 10 is added to a number, the tens-place digit increases by one.

Start at 2 and jump up 10.

$$2 + 10 = \underline{12}$$

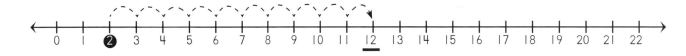

Start at 5 and jump up 10.

$$5 + 10 = \underline{\hspace{1cm}}$$

Start at 8 and jump up 10.

$$8 + 10 = \underline{\hspace{1cm}}$$

Start at 6 and jump up 10.

$$6 + 10 = \underline{\hspace{1cm}}$$

Complete the chart.

Number	Number + 10
2	12
5	
6	
8	

Building Math Fluency • EMC 3034 • © Evan-Moor Corp.

Name _____

Strategy

Plus Ten

When 10 is added to a number, the tens-place digit increases by one.

Use the number grid to help you add 10.
Shade the first number, and then shade where you land.
Write the answer.

(a) Start at 3 and add 10.

$$3 + 10 = \underline{13}$$

(b) Start at 13 and add 10.

$$13 + 10 = \underline{\hspace{1.5cm}}$$

(c) Start at 23 and add 10.

$$23 + 10 = \underline{\hspace{1.5cm}}$$

(d) Start at 33 and add 10.

$$33 + 10 = \underline{\hspace{1.5cm}}$$

(e) Start at 6 and add 10.

$$6 + 10 = \underline{\hspace{1.5cm}}$$

(f) Start at 16 and add 10.

$$16 + 10 = \underline{\hspace{1.5cm}}$$

(g) Start at _____ and add 10.

$$\underline{\hspace{1.5cm}} + 10 = \underline{\hspace{1.5cm}}$$

(h) Start at _____ and add 10.

$$\underline{\hspace{1.5cm}} + 10 = \underline{\hspace{1.5cm}}$$

1	2	3	4	5	6	7	8	9	10
11	12	13	14	15	16	17	18	19	20
21	22	23	24	25	26	27	28	29	30
31	32	33	34	35	36	37	38	39	40
41	42	43	44	45	46	47	48	49	50

Plus Ten

When 10 is added to a number, the tens-place digit increases by one.

Add 10 to each number.
Use the number grid to help you find the answer.

3 + 10 = _____   20 + 10 = _____

6 + 10 = _____   31 + 10 = _____

8 + 10 = _____   42 + 10 = _____

12 + 10 = _____   53 + 10 = _____

15 + 10 = _____   60 + 10 = _____

1	2	3	4	5	6	7	8	9	10
11	12	13	14	15	16	17	18	19	20
21	22	23	24	25	26	27	28	29	30
31	32	33	34	35	36	37	38	39	40
41	42	43	44	45	46	47	48	49	50
51	52	53	54	55	56	57	58	59	60
61	62	63	64	65	66	67	68	69	70

32 **Addition**   Building Math Fluency • EMC 3034 • © Evan-Moor Corp.

Strategy

Plus Ten

Jump 10. It's faster than counting by ones.

$2 + 10 = \underline{12}$

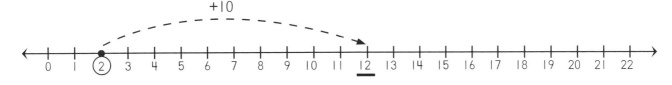

Jump 10 each time. Show it on the number lines.

$13 + 10 = \underline{\hspace{1.5cm}}$

$44 + 10 = \underline{\hspace{1.5cm}}$

Write your own equations. Use the number lines.

$\underline{\hspace{1.5cm}} + 10 = \underline{\hspace{1.5cm}}$

$\underline{\hspace{1.5cm}} + 10 = \underline{\hspace{1.5cm}}$

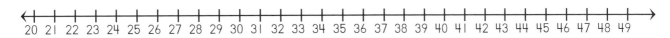

Strategy

Plus Ten

When 10 is added to a number, the tens-place digit increases by one.

Add 10 to each number. Fill in the chart.

Number	Number + 10
2	12
4	
5	
6	
8	
	19
	20
12	

Number	Number + 10
13	
	25
	30
	40
45	
90	
95	
100	

Think! What happens when 10 is added to a number?
What part of the number changes and what part stays the same?

_____

_____

_____

—— Word Box ——

digit   increase   add ten   ones place   tens place

Note: You may want to provide a number grid or number line to help students complete the chart.

Strategy

Plus Nine

See 9. Think 10.
When adding 9 to a number,
add 10 and jump back one.

7 + 9 = __16__

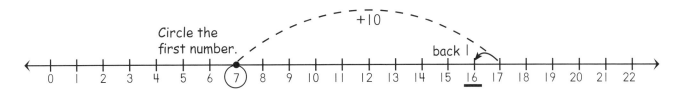

Circle the
first number.

+10

back 1

Use the number line to find the answer.

3 + 9 = _____

5 + 9 = _____

8 + 9 = _____

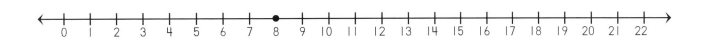

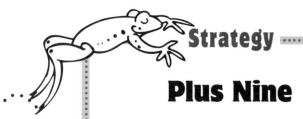

Name _____

See 9. Think 10.
When adding 9 to a number, add 10 and jump back one.

See 9. Think 10.
Add.

$6 + 9 =$ _____

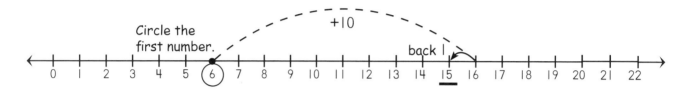

Circle the first number.

+10

back 1

$4 + 9 =$ _____

$12 + 9 =$ _____

$15 + 9 =$ _____

Building Math Fluency • EMC 3034 • © Evan-Moor Corp.

Strategy
Plus Nine

See 9. Think 10.
When adding 9 to a number,
add 10 and jump back one.

See 9. Think 10.
Solve and match.

$3 + 9$ $6 + 10 - 1 =$ _____

$6 + 9$ $3 + 10 - 1 =$ _____

$8 + 9$ $7 + 10 - 1 =$ _____

$7 + 9$ $8 + 10 - 1 =$ _____

$5 + 9$ $24 + 10 - 1 =$ _____

$13 + 9$ $5 + 10 - 1 =$ _____

$24 + 9$ $13 + 10 - 1 =$ _____

Strategy

Plus Nine

See 9. Think 10.
When adding 9 to a number,
add 10 and jump back one.

See 9. Think 10. Add.

$5 + 9$ is the same as $\underline{5 + 10 - 1} = \underline{14}$

$9 + 9$ is the same as $\underline{9 + 10 - 1} = \underline{}$

$7 + 9$ is the same as $\underline{} = \underline{}$

$4 + 9$ is the same as $\underline{} = \underline{}$

$8 + 9$ is the same as $\underline{} = \underline{}$

$16 + 9$ is the same as $\underline{} = \underline{}$

$23 + 9$ is the same as $\underline{} = \underline{}$

Write and solve **Plus Nine** problems.

_____   _____

_____   _____

Building Math Fluency • EMC 3034 • © Evan-Moor Corp.

Name _____

Strategy
Plus Nine

See 9. Make 10.
Another way to add 9 to a number is to make the 9 a 10 by reducing the other addend by one.

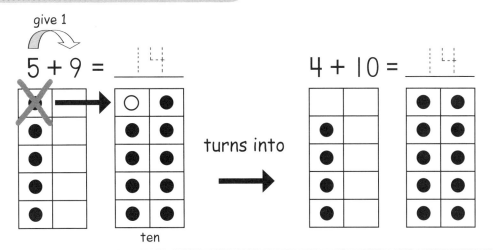

give 1

$5 + 9 = \underline{14}$ $4 + 10 = \underline{14}$

ten   turns into

Try it. Draw dots to show the new numbers.

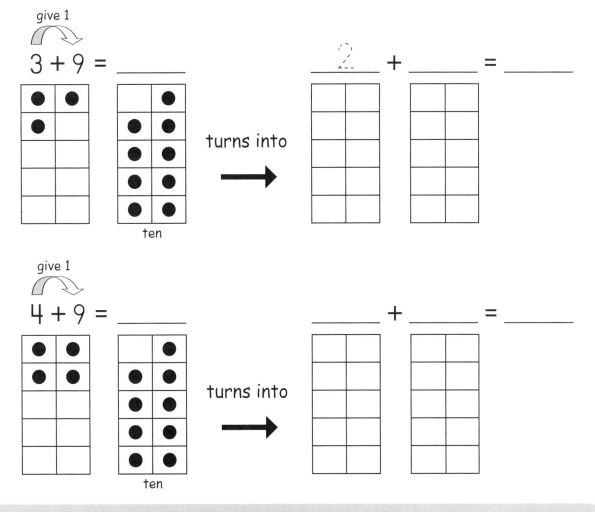

give 1

$3 + 9 = \underline{\hspace{1cm}}$ $\underline{2} + \underline{\hspace{1cm}} = \underline{\hspace{1cm}}$

ten   turns into

give 1

$4 + 9 = \underline{\hspace{1cm}}$ $\underline{\hspace{1cm}} + \underline{\hspace{1cm}} = \underline{\hspace{1cm}}$

ten   turns into

Strategy

Plus Nine

See 9. Make 10.
Another way to add 9 to a number
is to make the 9 a 10 by reducing
the other addend by one.

Complete the problems. Draw dots to show the new numbers.

Take one and give it to the 9.

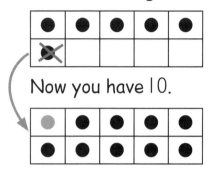

Now you have 10.

$$\begin{array}{r} 6 \\ + 9 \\ \hline \square \end{array}$$

⟷

$$\begin{array}{r} \boxed{5} \\ + 10 \\ \hline \boxed{15} \end{array}$$

Take one and give it to the 9.

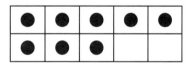

Now you have 10.

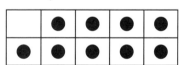

$$\begin{array}{r} 8 \\ + 9 \\ \hline \square \end{array}$$

⟷

$$\begin{array}{r} \square \\ + 10 \\ \hline \square \end{array}$$

Take one and give it to the 9.

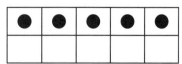

Now you have 10.

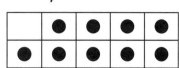

$$\begin{array}{r} 5 \\ + 9 \\ \hline \square \end{array}$$

⟷

$$\begin{array}{r} \square \\ + 10 \\ \hline \square \end{array}$$

40 **Addition**

Building Math Fluency • EMC 3034 • © Evan-Moor Corp.

Strategy

Plus Nine

See 9. Make 10.
Another way to add 9 to a number is to make the 9 a 10 by reducing the other addend by one.

Turn each **Plus Nine** problem into a **Plus Ten** problem.

give 1

$4 + 9$ turns into _____ + 10 = _____

give 1

$7 + 9$ turns into _____ + 10 = _____

give 1

$8 + 9$ turns into _____ + 10 = _____

$6 + 9$ turns into _____ + 10 = _____

$3 + 9$ turns into _____ + 10 = _____

$11 + 9$ turns into _____ + 10 = _____

The pattern I notice is _____

_____

Name _____

Strategy

Plus Nine

See 9. Make 10.
Another way to add 9 to a number
is to make the 9 a 10 by reducing
the other addend by one.

Turn each **Plus Nine** problem into a **Plus Ten** problem.

$5 + 9$ turns into   ___4 + 10___ = _____

$9 + 9$ turns into   ___8 + 10___ = _____

$2 + 9$ turns into   _____ = _____

$12 + 9$ turns into   _____ = _____

$13 + 9$ turns into   _____ = _____

$24 + 9$ turns into   _____ = _____

$6 + 9$ turns into   _____ = _____

$16 + 9$ turns into   _____ = _____

This strategy is: ❏ confusing   ❏ fun   ❏ difficult
(please check)
❏ easy   ❏ _____
other

Mixed Strategies Practice

Doubles and More

Circle the **Doubles** facts.
Then solve the problems.

$$
\begin{array}{r} 4 \\ + 4 \\ \hline 8 \end{array}
\qquad
\begin{array}{r} 8 \\ + 1 \\ \hline \end{array}
\qquad
\begin{array}{r} 5 \\ + 5 \\ \hline \end{array}
\qquad
\begin{array}{r} 5 \\ + 6 \\ \hline \end{array}
\qquad
\begin{array}{r} 3 \\ + 6 \\ \hline \end{array}
$$

$$
\begin{array}{r} 2 \\ + 8 \\ \hline \end{array}
\qquad
\begin{array}{r} 7 \\ + 7 \\ \hline \end{array}
\qquad
\begin{array}{r} 2 \\ + 2 \\ \hline \end{array}
\qquad
\begin{array}{r} 4 \\ + 5 \\ \hline \end{array}
\qquad
\begin{array}{r} 3 \\ + 3 \\ \hline \end{array}
$$

$$
\begin{array}{r} 6 \\ + 6 \\ \hline \end{array}
\qquad
\begin{array}{r} 8 \\ + 8 \\ \hline \end{array}
\qquad
\begin{array}{r} 7 \\ + 3 \\ \hline \end{array}
\qquad
\begin{array}{r} 9 \\ + 9 \\ \hline \end{array}
\qquad
\begin{array}{r} 4 \\ + 6 \\ \hline \end{array}
$$

Think about **Doubles**. Solve the problems.

$1 + 1 =$ _____ $10 + 10 =$ _____ $100 + 100 =$ _____

$2 + 2 =$ _____ $20 + 20 =$ _____ $200 + 200 =$ _____

$3 + 3 =$ _____ $30 + 30 =$ _____ $300 + 300 =$ _____

Name _____

Which Strategy Fits?

Cut and glue the facts under the best strategy.

Plus Zero Add 0 to a number and the number stays the same.	**Count Up** +1, +2, +3 Count up from the larger number. Add on 1, 2, or 3.

$8 + 1$	$0 + 10$	$6 + 2$
$6 + 0$	$4 + 3$	$9 + 0$
$9 + 3$	$0 + 7$	

Building Math Fluency • EMC 3034 • © Evan-Moor Corp.

Name _____

Which Strategy Fits?

Cut and glue the facts under the best strategy.

Doubles Add the number to itself.	**Doubles Plus One** Double the number. Add one more.

5 + 6	9 + 9	4 + 4
3 + 3	8 + 9	3 + 4
4 + 5	8 + 8	

Name _____

Which Strategy Fits?

Cut and glue the facts under the best strategy.

Plus Nine

See 9. Think 10. Then go back one.	**See 9 Make 10.** Then reduce the other addend by one.

$6 + 9$
$(5 + 10)$

$38 + 9$
$(38 + 10 - 1)$

$7 + 9$
$(7 + 10 - 1)$

$5 + 9$
$(4 + 10)$

$12 + 9$
$(12 + 10 - 1)$

$8 + 9$
$(7 + 10)$

$4 + 9$
$(3 + 10)$

$24 + 9$
$(24 + 10 - 1)$

Name _____

Add and Color

Find the problems that you would solve using each strategy.
Solve. Shade the boxes with the correct color.

Plus Zero—yellow   **Count Up**—orange   **Doubles**—red

+	0	1	2	3	4	5	6	7	8	9	10
0	0+0	0+1	0+2	0+3	0+4	0+5	0+6	0+7	0+8	0+9	0+10
1	1+0	1+1	1+2	1+3	1+4	1+5	1+6	1+7	1+8	1+9	1+10
2	2+0	2+1	2+2	2+3	2+4	2+5	2+6	2+7	2+8	2+9	2+10
3	3+0	3+1	3+2	3+3	3+4	3+5	3+6	3+7	3+8	3+9	3+10
4	4+0	4+1	4+2	4+3	4+4	4+5	4+6	4+7	4+8	4+9	4+10
5	5+0	5+1	5+2	5+3	5+4	5+5	5+6	5+7	5+8	5+9	5+10
6	6+0	6+1	6+2	6+3	6+4	6+5	6+6	6+7	6+8	6+9	6+10
7	7+0	7+1	7+2	7+3	7+4	7+5	7+6	7+7	7+8	7+9	7+10
8	8+0	8+1	8+2	8+3	8+4	8+5	8+6	8+7	8+8	8+9	8+10
9	9+0	9+1	9+2	9+3	9+4	9+5	9+6	9+7	9+8	9+9	9+10
10	10+0	10+1	10+2	10+3	10+4	10+5	10+6	10+7	10+8	10+9	10+10

Name _____

Color by Strategy

Find the problems that you would solve using each strategy.
Solve. Shade the boxes with the correct color.

Tens Partners—yellow   **Plus Ten**—blue   **Plus Nine**—green

+	0	1	2	3	4	5	6	7	8	9	10
0	0+0	0+1	0+2	0+3	0+4	0+5	0+6	0+7	0+8	0+9	0+10
1	1+0	1+1	1+2	1+3	1+4	1+5	1+6	1+7	1+8	1+9	1+10
2	2+0	2+1	2+2	2+3	2+4	2+5	2+6	2+7	2+8	2+9	2+10
3	3+0	3+1	3+2	3+3	3+4	3+5	3+6	3+7	3+8	3+9	3+10
4	4+0	4+1	4+2	4+3	4+4	4+5	4+6	4+7	4+8	4+9	4+10
5	5+0	5+1	5+2	5+3	5+4	5+5	5+6	5+7	5+8	5+9	5+10
6	6+0	6+1	6+2	6+3	6+4	6+5	6+6	6+7	6+8	6+9	6+10
7	7+0	7+1	7+2	7+3	7+4	7+5	7+6	7+7	7+8	7+9	7+10
8	8+0	8+1	8+2	8+3	8+4	8+5	8+6	8+7	8+8	8+9	8+10
9	9+0	9+1	9+2	9+3	9+4	9+5	9+6	9+7	9+8	9+9	9+10
10	10+0	10+1	10+2	10+3	10+4	10+5	10+6	10+7	10+8	10+9	10+10

Name _____

What's Your Strategy?

Find the problems that you would solve using each strategy.
Solve. Shade the boxes with the correct color.

Doubles — purple **Doubles Plus One** — blue **Tens Partners** — green

+	0	1	2	3	4	5	6	7	8	9	10
0	0+0	0+1	0+2	0+3	0+4	0+5	0+6	0+7	0+8	0+9	0+10
1	1+0	1+1	1+2	1+3	1+4	1+5	1+6	1+7	1+8	1+9	1+10
2	2+0	2+1	2+2	2+3	2+4	2+5	2+6	2+7	2+8	2+9	2+10
3	3+0	3+1	3+2	3+3	3+4	3+5	3+6	3+7	3+8	3+9	3+10
4	4+0	4+1	4+2	4+3	4+4	4+5	4+6	4+7	4+8	4+9	4+10
5	5+0	5+1	5+2	5+3	5+4	5+5	5+6	5+7	5+8	5+9	5+10
6	6+0	6+1	6+2	6+3	6+4	6+5	6+6	6+7	6+8	6+9	6+10
7	7+0	7+1	7+2	7+3	7+4	7+5	7+6	7+7	7+8	7+9	7+10
8	8+0	8+1	8+2	8+3	8+4	8+5	8+6	8+7	8+8	8+9	8+10
9	9+0	9+1	9+2	9+3	9+4	9+5	9+6	9+7	9+8	9+9	9+10
10	10+0	10+1	10+2	10+3	10+4	10+5	10+6	10+7	10+8	10+9	10+10

Name _____

Addition

Strategy Names

Count Up   Tens Partners   Doubles

Doubles Plus One   Plus Nine   Plus Ten

Complete each series. Write the strategy name.

Strategy name
Count Up

8 + 1 = _____

9 + 3 = _____

14 + 2 = _____

19 + 1 = _____

15 + 2 = _____

11 + 3 = _____

Strategy name

9 + 9 = _____

8 + 8 = _____

7 + 7 = _____

6 + 6 = _____

5 + 5 = _____

10 + 10 = _____

Strategy name

0 + 10 = _____

8 + 2 = _____

4 + 6 = _____

5 + 5 = _____

7 + 3 = _____

1 + 9 = _____

Strategy name

3 + 4 = _____

4 + 5 = _____

5 + 6 = _____

7 + 8 = _____

8 + 9 = _____

9 + 10 = _____

Strategy name

8 + 10 = _____

9 + 10 = _____

7 + 10 = _____

5 + 10 = _____

6 + 10 = _____

11 + 10 = _____

Strategy name

8 + 9 = _____

9 + 9 = _____

7 + 9 = _____

5 + 9 = _____

6 + 9 = _____

4 + 9 = _____

Building Math Fluency • EMC 3034 • © Evan-Moor Corp.

Mixed Strategies Practice

Addition Power

Add and color.

9 + 9	3 + 4	8 + 2	7 + 8	10 + 8
5 + 1	9 + 3	6 + 9	12 + 7	4 + 4
1 + 9	6 + 8	8 + 8	6 + 0	6 + 3
7 + 5	14 + 5	3 + 5	4 + 5	7 + 7
13 + 7	2 + 7	3 + 7	7 + 6	16 + 2
6 + 2	4 + 6	6 + 6	11 + 8	4 + 2

If the sum is between	Color the square
0 and 8	yellow
9 and 11	red
12 and 15	green
16 and 20	blue

Teaching Subtraction Strategies

Pages 54–76 present practice with subtraction strategies that promote computational fluency and fact mastery.

There are two ways to look at subtraction:

- as the comparison of two quantities
"The difference between 16 and 7 is 9."

- as the changing of an amount to less
"If I take 7 away from 16, I have 9 left."

$$16 - 7 = 9$$

Minus Zero means subtract 0 from any number and the number stays the same.

$$3 - 0 = 3$$

A Number Minus Itself means a number subtracted from itself is 0.

$$5 - 5 = 0 \qquad 8 - 8 = 0 \qquad 3 - 3 = 0$$

Count Back to take away small numbers, such as 1, 2, or 3.

$$4 - 1 = 3 \qquad 4 - 2 = 2 \qquad 4 - 3 = 1$$

Count Up to find the difference. This strategy is best when the numbers are close together.

$$11 - 9 = 2 \quad \text{Count up two from 9 to 11.}$$

Think Addition means that every subtraction fact is the reverse of an addition fact.

$$6 + 2 = 8 \quad so \quad 8 - 2 = 6$$

Tens Partners are helpful because if you know the addition pairs, then you know the related subtraction facts.

$$7 + 3 = 10 \quad so \quad 10 - 3 = 7 \quad and \quad 10 - 7 = 3$$

Doubles are helpful because if you know the addition doubles, then you know the related subtraction facts.

$$8 + 8 = 16 \quad so \quad 16 - 8 = 8$$

Minus Ten means that when 10 is subtracted from a number, the tens-place digit decreases by one, while the ones-place digit stays the same.

$$30 - 10 = 20$$

Minus Nine is based on the fact that 9 is one away from 10. Two common approaches are:

See 9. Think 10. Subtract 10 and add 1.	See 9 Make 10. Increase each number by one.
See $12 - 9$ Think $12 - 10 + 1$.	Turn $12 - 9$ into $13 - 10$

Building Math Fluency • EMC 3034 • © Evan-Moor Corp.

Subtraction Strategies

Minus Zero	Subtract 0 from a number and the number stays the same. $8 - 0 = 8$
A Number Minus Itself	Subtract a number from itself and the result is 0. $8 - 8 = 0$
Count Back $-1, -2, -3$	Count back to take away small numbers, such as 1, 2, or 3. $17 - 1 = 16$ $17 - 2 = 15$ $17 - 3 = 14$
Count Up	Count up to find the difference when the numbers are close together. $17 - 15 = 2$ Count up two from 15 to 17.
Think Addition	To subtract, think of the related addition fact. $8 + 6 = 14$ so $14 - 6 = 8$
Tens Partners	If you know the Tens Partners, then you know the related subtraction facts. $7 + 3 = 10$ so $10 - 7 = 3$
Doubles	If you know the addition doubles, then you know the related subtraction facts. $6 + 6 = 12$ so $12 - 6 = 6$
Minus Ten	Subtract 10 and the tens-place digit decreases by one, while the ones-place digit stays the same. $30 - 10 = 20$

Minus Nine
 	
    See 9. Think 10.
 	
    See 9. Make 10.
	Remember that 9 is just one away from 10. Two common approaches are:
	
	See 9. Think 10. Subtract 10 and add 1.
	See $12 - 9$. Think $12 - 10 + 1$.
	
	See 9. Make 10. Increase each number by one.
	Turn $12 - 9$ into $13 - 10$.

Strategy

Minus Zero

Subtract 0 and the number stays the same.

$$4 - 0 = 4$$

Subtract 0.

$5 - 0 = \boxed{}$ $8 - 0 = \boxed{}$

$9 - 0 = \boxed{}$ $14 - 0 = \boxed{}$

$5 - \boxed{} = 5$ $12 - \boxed{} = 12$

Find the difference.

$105 - 0 = \boxed{}$ $99 - 0 = \boxed{}$

$321 - 0 = \boxed{}$ $56 - 0 = \boxed{}$

Write your own **Minus Zero** problems.

$$\begin{array}{c} \boxed{} \\ -\ 0 \\ \hline \boxed{} \end{array} \qquad \begin{array}{c} \boxed{} \\ -\ 0 \\ \hline \boxed{} \end{array} \qquad \begin{array}{c} \boxed{} \\ -\ 0 \\ \hline \boxed{} \end{array}$$

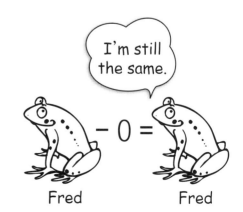

I'm still the same.

$- 0 =$

Fred   Fred

Building Math Fluency • EMC 3034 • © Evan-Moor Corp.

Strategy

A Number Minus Itself

Subtract a number from itself and the result is 0.

$$8 - 8 = 0$$

Subtract the number from itself.

$5 - 5 = \boxed{}$ $9 - 9 = \boxed{}$

$7 - 7 = \boxed{}$ $12 - 12 = \boxed{}$

$3 - \boxed{} = 0$ $15 - \boxed{} = 0$

Write problems in which the difference is 0.

$\boxed{} - \boxed{} = 0$ $\boxed{} - \boxed{} = 0$

$\boxed{} - \boxed{} = 0$ $\boxed{} - \boxed{} = 0$

$$\begin{array}{r} \boxed{} \\ -\ \boxed{} \\ \hline 0 \end{array}\qquad \begin{array}{r} \boxed{} \\ -\ \boxed{} \\ \hline 0 \end{array}\qquad \begin{array}{r} \boxed{} \\ -\ \boxed{} \\ \hline 0 \end{array}$$

Strategy
Count Back
−1, −2, −3

Count Back to take away small numbers, such as 1, 2, or 3.

$$5 - 3 = 2$$

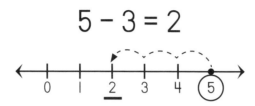

Use the number line to **Count Back**.

Start at 11 and count back 2.

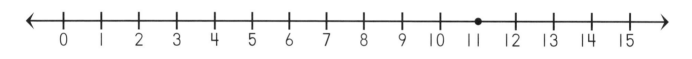

$$11 - 2 = \underline{\hspace{2cm}}$$

Start at 9 and count back 3.

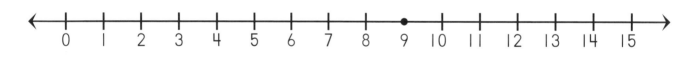

$$9 - 3 = \underline{\hspace{2cm}}$$

Start at 14 and count back 2.

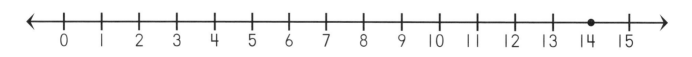

$$14 - 2 = \underline{\hspace{2cm}}$$

Building Math Fluency • EMC 3034 • © Evan-Moor Corp.

Strategy
Count Back
-1, -2, -3

Count Back to take away small numbers, such as 1, 2, or 3.

Count Back to find the difference.
Use the number line if you like.

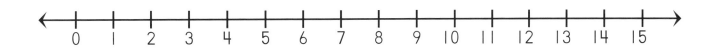

$$0 \quad 1 \quad 2 \quad 3 \quad 4 \quad 5 \quad 6 \quad 7 \quad 8 \quad 9 \quad 10 \quad 11 \quad 12 \quad 13 \quad 14 \quad 15$$

6 – 1 = _____   11 – 3 = _____   14 – 3 = _____

15 – 1 = _____   9 – 2 = _____   12 – 3 = _____

14 – 2 = _____   6 – 3 = _____   3 – 2 = _____

5	15	4	10	6	6
– 2	– 2	– 3	– 1	– 0	– 2

Count Back in your head. Write the difference.

11 – 2 = _____   13 – 2 = _____   8 – 2 = _____

17 – 2 = _____   9 – 3 = _____   15 – 3 = _____

Strategy
Count Back
-1, -2, -3

Count Back to take away small numbers, such as 1, 2, or 3.

Count Back to subtract.
Use the number line if you like.

16 – 2 = ☐   8 – 3 = ☐

22 – 1 = ☐   19 – 2 = ☐

11 – 3 = ☐   14 – 1 = ☐

Complete the equations.

22 – ☐ = 20   17 – ☐ = 16

10 – ☐ = 7   15 – ☐ = 12

8 – ☐ = 6   18 – ☐ = 16

13 – ☐ = 10   16 – ☐ = 14

Write your own equations.

☐ – 2 = ☐   ☐ – 3 = ☐

☐ – 1 = ☐   ☐ – 2 = ☐

Number line (right side):
22, 21, 20, 19, 18, 17, 16, 15, 14, 13, 12, 11, 10, 9, 8, 7, 6, 5, 4, 3, 2, 1, 0

Building Math Fluency • EMC 3034 • © Evan-Moor Corp.

Strategy

Count Up

Count Up to find the difference between the numbers.

Start at 9. **Count Up** to 11.
The number of hops is the difference.

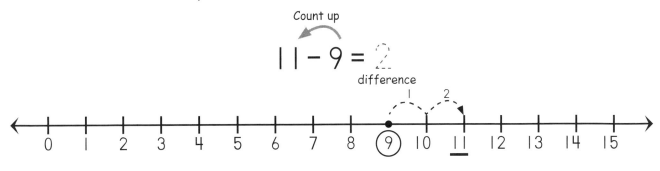

Count up

$11 - 9 = 2$

difference

Use the number line to **Count Up**.

Start at 12. Count up to 15.
The number of hops is the difference.

$$15 - 12 = \underline{\qquad}$$

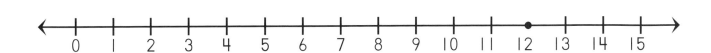

Start at 9. Count up to 12.
The number of hops is the difference.

$$12 - 9 = \underline{\qquad}$$

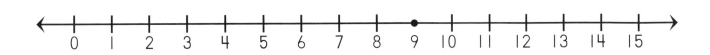

Subtraction 59

Strategy

Count Up

Count Up to find the difference.

Use the number line to **Count Up**. Solve.

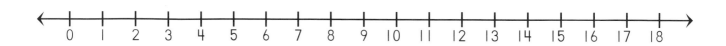

0 1 2 3 4 5 6 7 8 9 10 11 12 13 14 15 16 17 18

$5 - 4 =$ _____ $9 - 8 =$ _____ $16 - 15 =$ _____

$15 - 4 =$ _____ $14 - 12 =$ _____ $12 - 11 =$ _____

Count Up from the bottom number with tally marks. Solve.

$\begin{array}{r} 11 \\ -\ 9 \\ \hline \end{array}$ // $\begin{array}{r} 18 \\ -16 \\ \hline \end{array}$ $\begin{array}{r} 18 \\ -15 \\ \hline \end{array}$ $\begin{array}{r} 5 \\ -\ 3 \\ \hline \end{array}$

$\begin{array}{r} 15 \\ -12 \\ \hline \end{array}$ /// $\begin{array}{r} 12 \\ -10 \\ \hline \end{array}$ $\begin{array}{r} 7 \\ -\ 5 \\ \hline \end{array}$ $\begin{array}{r} 15 \\ -14 \\ \hline \end{array}$

Count Up with dots. Solve.

14,15
• •
$15 - 13 = \underline{2}$

9,10,11
• • •
$11 - 8 = \underline{3}$ $9 - 7 =$ _____

$13 - 11 =$ _____ $8 - 6 =$ _____ $17 - 16 =$ _____

   Building Math Fluency • EMC 3034 • © Evan-Moor Corp.

Strategy

Which Strategy Fits?

Count Back

Count back when subtracting a small number. **Count Back** works for −1, −2, −3 problems.

$$100 - 2 = \underline{98}$$

It is fast to count back 2.

Count Up

Count up when subtracting a large number. **Count Up** works best when the numbers in the problem are close together.

$$100 - 99 = \underline{1}$$

It is too far to count back 99. It is easy to count up from 99.

Circle **Count Back** problems in blue.
Circle **Count Up** problems in red.
Solve.

$20 - 1 = \underline{\hspace{1cm}}$ $20 - 18 = \underline{\hspace{1cm}}$ $20 - 3 = \underline{\hspace{1cm}}$

$14 - 2 = \underline{\hspace{1cm}}$ $14 - 11 = \underline{\hspace{1cm}}$ $13 - 2 = \underline{\hspace{1cm}}$

$9 - 1 = \underline{\hspace{1cm}}$ $19 - 1 = \underline{\hspace{1cm}}$ $19 - 16 = \underline{\hspace{1cm}}$

Bonus problems:

$80 - 1 = \underline{\hspace{1cm}}$ $80 - 76 = \underline{\hspace{1cm}}$ $95 - 3 = \underline{\hspace{1cm}}$

$99 - 2 = \underline{\hspace{1cm}}$ $59 - 58 = \underline{\hspace{1cm}}$ $41 - 40 = \underline{\hspace{1cm}}$

Strategy

Think Addition

Every subtraction problem can be solved as addition.

$7 - 5 = \boxed{2}$ is the same as $2 + \boxed{5} = 7$

Solve the subtraction problem. Rewrite it as an addition problem.

Subtraction		Addition
Add $12 - 9 = \boxed{3}$	➡	$3 + \boxed{} = 12$
$11 - 7 = \boxed{}$	➡	$4 + \boxed{} = 11$
$13 - 8 = \boxed{}$	➡	$\boxed{} + \boxed{} = 13$
$14 - 7 = \boxed{}$	➡	$\boxed{} + \boxed{} = 14$
$15 - 9 = \boxed{}$	➡	$\boxed{} + \boxed{} = 15$
$11 - 5 = \boxed{}$	➡	$6 + \boxed{} = 11$
$12 - 7 = \boxed{}$	➡	$5 + \boxed{} = 12$

Building Math Fluency • EMC 3034 • © Evan-Moor Corp.

 **Strategy**

Think Addition

Name _____

Every subtraction problem can be solved as addition.

Use addition to solve subtraction.
Solve and match.

4 + 6 = __10__   10 – 5 = _____

2 + 8 = _____   10 – 6 = __4__

3 + 7 = _____   10 – 8 = _____

1 + 9 = _____   10 – 9 = _____

5 + 5 = _____   10 – 7 = _____

The above facts are: ❑ Tens Partners ❑ Doubles ❑ Plus Ten

5 + 5 = _____   12 – 6 = _____

6 + 6 = _____   14 – 7 = _____

7 + 7 = _____   16 – 8 = _____

8 + 8 = _____   10 – 5 = _____

9 + 9 = _____   18 – 9 = _____

The above facts are: ❑ Tens Partners ❑ Doubles ❑ Plus Ten

Name _____

Think Addition

Every subtraction problem
can be solved as addition.

Use addition to solve subtraction.

Add	Match	Subtract
4 + 4 = __8__		11 − 6 = _____
5 + 6 = _____		8 − 4 = __4__
7 + 7 = _____		14 − 7 = _____
7 + 8 = _____		12 − 3 = _____
9 + 3 = _____		16 − 2 = _____
14 + 2 = _____		15 − 8 = _____
17 + 3 = _____		20 − 3 = _____

Write three addition facts. Match them to the related subtraction facts.

Add	Match	Subtract
_____		_____
_____		_____
_____		_____

Building Math Fluency • EMC 3034 • © Evan-Moor Corp.

 **Strategy**

Tens Partners

If you know the **Tens Partners**, then you know the related subtraction facts.

Use the **Tens Partners** facts to solve subtraction.

2 + 8 = _____   so

$10 -$ _____ $= 2$

$10 -$ _____ $= 8$

7 + 3 = _____   so

$10 -$ _____ $= 7$

$10 -$ _____ $= 3$

9 + 1 = _____   so

$10 -$ _____ $= 9$

$10 -$ _____ $= 1$

6 + 4 = _____   so

$10 -$ _____ $= 6$

$10 -$ _____ $= 4$

5 + 5 = _____   so

$10 -$ _____ $= 5$

$10 - 5 =$ _____

 **Strategy**

Tens Partners

 Name _____

If you know the **Tens Partners**, then you know the related subtraction facts.

Do the addition facts. Then apply addition to subtraction facts.

Tens Partners Addition		Tens Partners Subtraction	
3 + 7	2 + 8	10 − 8	10 − 5
1 + 9	4 + 6	10 − 3	10 − 2
8 + 2	9 + 1	10 − 1	10 − 7
7 + 3	6 + 4	10 − 9	10 − 4
5 + 5	10 + 0	10 − 6	10 − 0

Name _____

Strategy

Doubles

If you know the addition **Doubles**, then you know the related subtraction facts.

Apply addition to subtraction facts.

2 + 2 = _____   so   4 − _____ = 2

3 + 3 = _____   so   6 − _____ = 3

4 + 4 = _____   so   8 − _____ = 4

5 + 5 = _____   so   10 − _____ = 5

6 + 6 = _____   so   12 − _____ = 6

7 + 7 = _____   so   14 − _____ = 7

8 + 8 = _____   so   16 − _____ = 8

9 + 9 = _____   so   18 − _____ = 9

Strategy

Doubles

If you know the addition **Doubles**, then you know the related subtraction facts.

Do the addition facts. Then use addition to solve the subtraction facts.

Doubles Addition

$$\begin{array}{r} 5 \\ + 5 \\ \hline \end{array} \qquad \begin{array}{r} 9 \\ + 9 \\ \hline \end{array}$$

$$\begin{array}{r} 8 \\ + 8 \\ \hline \end{array} \qquad \begin{array}{r} 3 \\ + 3 \\ \hline \end{array}$$

$$\begin{array}{r} 4 \\ + 4 \\ \hline \end{array} \qquad \begin{array}{r} 6 \\ + 6 \\ \hline \end{array}$$

$$\begin{array}{r} 7 \\ + 7 \\ \hline \end{array} \qquad \begin{array}{r} 2 \\ + 2 \\ \hline \end{array}$$

$$\begin{array}{r} 10 \\ + 10 \\ \hline \end{array} \qquad \begin{array}{r} 11 \\ + 11 \\ \hline \end{array}$$

Doubles Subtraction

$$\begin{array}{r} 10 \\ - 5 \\ \hline \end{array} \qquad \begin{array}{r} 20 \\ - 10 \\ \hline \end{array}$$

$$\begin{array}{r} 12 \\ - 6 \\ \hline \end{array} \qquad \begin{array}{r} 8 \\ - 4 \\ \hline \end{array}$$

$$\begin{array}{r} 14 \\ - 7 \\ \hline \end{array} \qquad \begin{array}{r} 4 \\ - 2 \\ \hline \end{array}$$

$$\begin{array}{r} 16 \\ - 8 \\ \hline \end{array} \qquad \begin{array}{r} 6 \\ - 3 \\ \hline \end{array}$$

$$\begin{array}{r} 18 \\ - 9 \\ \hline \end{array} \qquad \begin{array}{r} 22 \\ - 11 \\ \hline \end{array}$$

Building Math Fluency • EMC 3034 • © Evan-Moor Corp.

Answer Key

Page 8
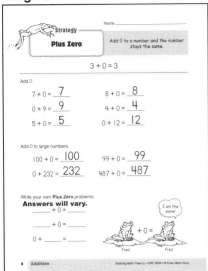

Page 9
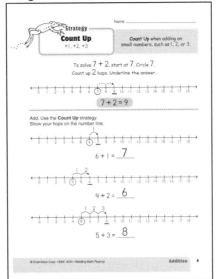

Page 10
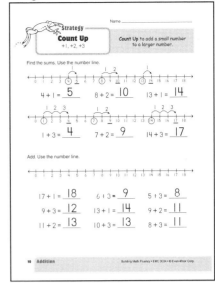

Page 11
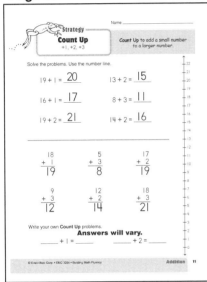

Page 12
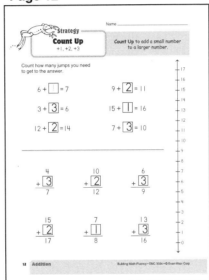

Page 13
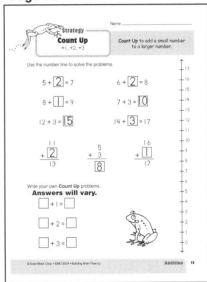

Page 14
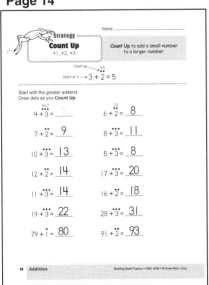

Page 15
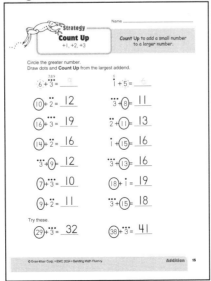

Page 16
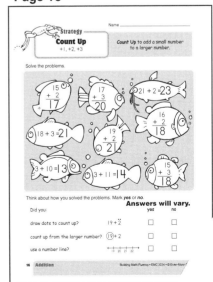

Strategy

Minus Ten

When you subtract 10, the tens-place digit decreases by one, and the ones-place digit stays the same.

Show $24 - 10 =$ ___14___

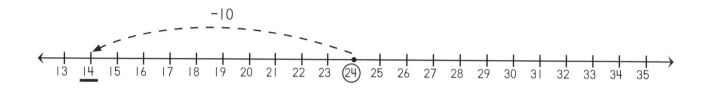

Jump back 10 on the number line.

Show $34 - 10 =$ _____

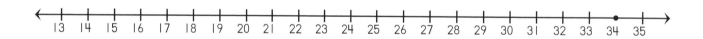

Show $61 - 10 =$ _____

Show $68 - 10 =$ _____

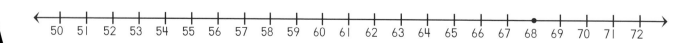

Building Math Fluency • EMC 3034 • © Evan-Moor Corp.

Strategy

Minus Nine

See 9. Think 10.

When subtracting 9 from a number, subtract 10 and then add 1.

Show $23 - 9 =$ ____ 14

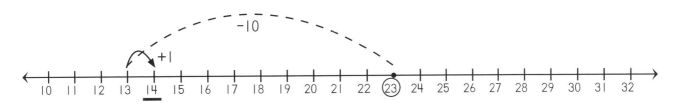

Jump back 10 and then go up one.
Use the number line.

$25 - 9 =$ _____ $30 - 9 =$ _____

$27 - 9 =$ _____ $34 - 9 =$ _____

Subtract.

15	18	14	19	16	13
$- 10$	$- 9$	$- 10$	$- 10$	$- 9$	$- 10$

Name ______________________________

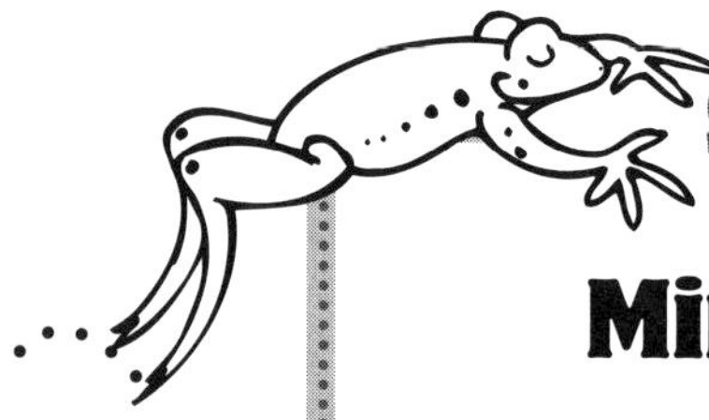

Strategy

Minus Nine

See 9. Make 10.
When subtracting 9 from a number, increase each number by one, and the difference stays the same.

Minus Nine		Minus Ten
17 − 9	is the same as	18 − 10 = 8
24 − 9	is the same as	25 − 10 = 15

Turn **Minus Nine** into **Minus Ten**. Solve.

15 − 9 → __16__ − 10 = ______

21 − 9 → __22__ − 10 = ______

25 − 9 → ______ − 10 = ______

33 − 9 → ______ − 10 = ______

27 − 9 → ______ − 10 = ______

55 − 9 → ______ − 10 = ______

44 − 9 → ______ − 10 = ______

22 − 9 → ______ − 10 = ______

Name _____

Subtraction

····· Strategy Names ·····

Count Back   ~~Count Up~~   A Number Minus Itself

Minus Ten   Doubles   Tens Partners

Complete each series.
Write the strategy name.

Strategy name

Count Up

20 – 18 = ____

14 – 13 = ____

19 – 17 = ____

11 – 9 = ____

12 – 8 = ____

18 – 16 = ____

Strategy name

10 – 4 = ____

10 – 8 = ____

10 – 7 = ____

10 – 5 = ____

10 – 3 = ____

10 – 9 = ____

Strategy name

9 – 9 = ____

8 – 8 = ____

4 – 4 = ____

5 – 5 = ____

7 – 7 = ____

1 – 1 = ____

Strategy name

13 – 1 = ____

20 – 2 = ____

15 – 2 = ____

19 – 3 = ____

11 – 2 = ____

16 – 1 = ____

Strategy name

18 – 10 = ____

19 – 10 = ____

17 – 10 = ____

15 – 10 = ____

16 – 10 = ____

20 – 10 = ____

Strategy name

18 – 9 = ____

16 – 8 = ____

14 – 7 = ____

12 – 6 = ____

8 – 4 = ____

6 – 3 = ____

Mixed Strategies Practice

Name _____

Which Strategy Fits?

Write each fact under the best strategy.
Solve the problems.

Count Back

A Number Minus Itself

Minus Zero

$10 - 0 = 10$

Minus Ten

Cross out the facts you use.

$10 - 0$ $10 - 10$ $12 - 0$

$16 - 1$ $18 - 2$ $14 - 10$

$19 - 10$ $18 - 18$ $12 - 3$

$15 - 15$ $13 - 0$ $17 - 10$

Building Math Fluency • EMC 3034 • © Evan-Moor Corp.

Mixed Strategies Practice

Name the Strategy

Write each fact under the best strategy.
Solve the problems.

Doubles

$6 - 3 = 3$

Tens Partners

Count Up

Cross out the facts you use.

7 – 5	8 – 4	15 – 14
12 – 6	~~6 – 3~~	10 – 9
10 – 6	9 – 6	13 – 11
14 – 7	10 – 7	18 – 9

Name _____

Subtraction Challenge

Subtract.

19 − 3	3 − 3	19 − 8	17 − 9	17 − 1
20 − 5	9 − 5	6 − 5	12 − 6	20 − 6
18 − 9	16 − 8	20 − 7	6 − 0	16 − 7
17 − 6	14 − 8	18 − 5	11 − 5	17 − 8
13 − 1	12 − 7	13 − 12	7 − 6	16 − 4
23 − 20	11 − 9	16 − 6	11 − 8	18 − 2

If the difference is between	Color the square
0 and 8	yellow
9 and 11	red
12 and 15	green
16 and 20	blue

Building Math Fluency • EMC 3034 • © Evan-Moor Corp.

How to Use
Test Your Skills

The *Test Your Skills* exercises on pages 80–107 provide multiple opportunities for assessment of computational skills. Each test series—for addition and subtraction—begins with easier problems and increases in difficulty.

Each page in the *Test Your Skills* section may be used multiple times and in different ways to build computational skills and improve fact fluency.

Mixed Strategies Practice

The tests provide the opportunity to practice many of the computational strategies presented in the first part of this book. For each problem, students should ask themselves: Which strategy best suits the numbers involved?

Strategy Focus

Have students select one strategy at a time to practice. They examine the problems and then circle and solve those that fit the focus strategy.

Assessment

Use the tests to determine how students are progressing in their acquisition of computational skills. If appropriate, allow students to set their own goals for improvement of computation speed.

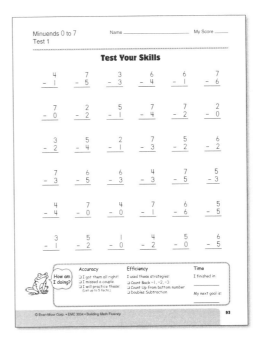

Student Self-Evaluation

The record area at the bottom of each *Test Your Skills* page affords students the opportunity to assess their own performance and use of computational strategies. This self-evaluation is an important part of the skill-building process.

Student Assessment/Record

Name

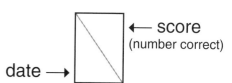
Test Levels	Addition—Sums						Subtraction—Minuends					
0 to 7												
7 to 10												
10 to 12												
13 to 15												
15 to 17												
15 to 20												
18 to 20												

Notes:

Building Math Fluency • EMC 3034 • © Evan-Moor Corp.

Class Assessment/Record

Students	Addition—Sums					Subtraction—Minuends					
	0 to 7	7 to 10	10 to 12	13 to 15	15 to 20	0 to 7	7 to 10	10 to 12	13 to 15	15 to 17	18 to 20

Name _____   My Score _____

Test Your Skills

```
    0         1         2         3         3         4
+   0     +   1     +   1     +   0     +   2     +   0
```

```
    4         4         5         5         1         6
+   2     +   3     +   1     +   2     +   5     +   1
```

```
    2         2         7         3         2         3
+   3     +   2     +   0     +   2     +   4     +   3
```

```
    1         2         3         3         2         4
+   0     +   0     +   3     +   1     +   2     +   1
```

```
    4         5         5         3         6         1
+   3     +   0     +   2     +   4     +   0     +   6
```

```
    2         4         1         7         2         4
+   5     +   2     +   3     +   0     +   3     +   3
```

How am I doing?

Accuracy
❑ I got them all right!
❑ I missed a couple.
❑ I will practice these:
   (List up to 4 facts.)

Efficiency
I used these strategies:
❑ Plus Zero
❑ Count Up +1, +2, +3
❑ Doubles/Doubles Plus One

Time
I finished in:

_____

My next goal is:

_____

Building Math Fluency • EMC 3034 • © Evan-Moor Corp.

Name _____   My Score _____

Test Your Skills

2 + 3	4 + 3	4 + 1	3 + 2	4 + 2	3 + 1
2 + 2	2 + 1	1 + 1	1 + 0	7 + 0	1 + 6
2 + 4	4 + 0	6 + 1	2 + 4	1 + 5	2 + 2
5 + 2	2 + 3	2 + 5	3 + 4	0 + 0	4 + 1
4 + 2	3 + 3	5 + 0	3 + 0	2 + 4	5 + 2
2 + 5	5 + 1	6 + 1	4 + 3	6 + 0	2 + 3

How am I doing?

Accuracy
❏ I got them all right!
❏ I missed a couple.
❏ I will practice these:
(List up to 4 facts.)

Efficiency
I used these strategies:
❏ Plus Zero
❏ Count Up +1, +2, +3
❏ Doubles/Doubles Plus One

Time
I finished in:

_____

My next goal is:

_____

Name _____   My Score _____

Test Your Skills

10 + 0	8 + 2	6 + 4	4 + 6	9 + 0	6 + 2
9 + 1	7 + 3	5 + 5	2 + 7	1 + 9	8 + 1
8 + 2	4 + 5	6 + 3	4 + 3	7 + 2	5 + 3
8 + 1	5 + 3	2 + 5	1 + 7	6 + 1	2 + 8
9 + 1	4 + 4	3 + 6	0 + 8	4 + 6	3 + 4
3 + 7	4 + 5	3 + 5	2 + 7	5 + 4	9 + 0

How am I doing?

Accuracy
❏ I got them all right!
❏ I missed a couple.
❏ I will practice these:
  (List up to 4 facts.)

Efficiency
I used these strategies:
❏ Plus Zero
❏ Count Up +1, +2, +3
❏ Doubles/Doubles Plus One
❏ Tens Partners

Time
I finished in:
_____

My next goal is:
_____

Name _____   My Score _____

Test Your Skills

5 + 4	1 + 9	3 + 5	10 + 0	6 + 3	9 + 0
8 + 2	4 + 5	3 + 7	6 + 4	5 + 5	3 + 4
8 + 0	7 + 2	4 + 4	6 + 1	2 + 8	5 + 3
5 + 4	2 + 7	3 + 6	9 + 1	8 + 0	8 + 2
3 + 4	2 + 6	5 + 5	7 + 0	4 + 3	7 + 3
8 + 1	3 + 6	5 + 2	1 + 7	2 + 5	2 + 8

How am I doing?

Accuracy
❑ I got them all right!
❑ I missed a couple.
❑ I will practice these:
(List up to 4 facts.)

Efficiency
I used these strategies:
❑ Plus Zero
❑ Count Up +1, +2, +3
❑ Doubles/Doubles Plus One
❑ Tens Partners

Time
I finished in:
_____
My next goal is:
_____

Name _____   My Score _____

Test Your Skills

$$
\begin{array}{r} 8 \\ + 2 \\ \hline \end{array}
\qquad
\begin{array}{r} 3 \\ + 4 \\ \hline \end{array}
\qquad
\begin{array}{r} 5 \\ + 5 \\ \hline \end{array}
\qquad
\begin{array}{r} 3 \\ + 6 \\ \hline \end{array}
\qquad
\begin{array}{r} 2 \\ + 7 \\ \hline \end{array}
\qquad
\begin{array}{r} 1 \\ + 8 \\ \hline \end{array}
$$

$$
\begin{array}{r} 9 \\ + 0 \\ \hline \end{array}
\qquad
\begin{array}{r} 7 \\ + 2 \\ \hline \end{array}
\qquad
\begin{array}{r} 5 \\ + 3 \\ \hline \end{array}
\qquad
\begin{array}{r} 9 \\ + 1 \\ \hline \end{array}
\qquad
\begin{array}{r} 4 \\ + 5 \\ \hline \end{array}
\qquad
\begin{array}{r} 6 \\ + 3 \\ \hline \end{array}
$$

$$
\begin{array}{r} 2 \\ + 7 \\ \hline \end{array}
\qquad
\begin{array}{r} 6 \\ + 4 \\ \hline \end{array}
\qquad
\begin{array}{r} 8 \\ + 0 \\ \hline \end{array}
\qquad
\begin{array}{r} 8 \\ + 2 \\ \hline \end{array}
\qquad
\begin{array}{r} 4 \\ + 3 \\ \hline \end{array}
\qquad
\begin{array}{r} 5 \\ + 5 \\ \hline \end{array}
$$

$$
\begin{array}{r} 2 \\ + 6 \\ \hline \end{array}
\qquad
\begin{array}{r} 8 \\ + 1 \\ \hline \end{array}
\qquad
\begin{array}{r} 6 \\ + 3 \\ \hline \end{array}
\qquad
\begin{array}{r} 7 \\ + 3 \\ \hline \end{array}
\qquad
\begin{array}{r} 2 \\ + 5 \\ \hline \end{array}
\qquad
\begin{array}{r} 4 \\ + 4 \\ \hline \end{array}
$$

$$
\begin{array}{r} 7 \\ + 3 \\ \hline \end{array}
\qquad
\begin{array}{r} 4 \\ + 5 \\ \hline \end{array}
\qquad
\begin{array}{r} 9 \\ + 1 \\ \hline \end{array}
\qquad
\begin{array}{r} 4 \\ + 2 \\ \hline \end{array}
\qquad
\begin{array}{r} 6 \\ + 2 \\ \hline \end{array}
\qquad
\begin{array}{r} 5 \\ + 1 \\ \hline \end{array}
$$

$$
\begin{array}{r} 5 \\ + 2 \\ \hline \end{array}
\qquad
\begin{array}{r} 4 \\ + 3 \\ \hline \end{array}
\qquad
\begin{array}{r} 5 \\ + 4 \\ \hline \end{array}
\qquad
\begin{array}{r} 3 \\ + 2 \\ \hline \end{array}
\qquad
\begin{array}{r} 3 \\ + 7 \\ \hline \end{array}
\qquad
\begin{array}{r} 2 \\ + 8 \\ \hline \end{array}
$$

How am I doing?

Accuracy
❏ I got them all right!
❏ I missed a couple.
❏ I will practice these:
   (List up to 4 facts.)

Efficiency
I used these strategies:
❏ Plus Zero
❏ Count Up +1, +2, +3
❏ Doubles/Doubles Plus One
❏ Tens Partners

Time
I finished in:
_____

My next goal is:
_____

Name _____   My Score _____

Test Your Skills

10 + 0	10 + 2	6 + 4	9 + 2	3 + 8	6 + 6
11 + 1	7 + 3	5 + 5	4 + 8	9 + 1	12 + 0
8 + 3	7 + 5	3 + 7	10 + 2	2 + 9	4 + 7
10 + 1	9 + 3	6 + 5	4 + 8	5 + 7	11 + 0
7 + 4	6 + 6	8 + 4	2 + 8	12 + 0	2 + 9
6 + 4	10 + 1	7 + 5	3 + 7	10 + 2	4 + 7

How am I doing?

Accuracy
❑ I got them all right!
❑ I missed a couple.
❑ I will practice these:
(List up to 4 facts.)

Efficiency
I used these strategies:
❑ Count Up +1, +2, +3
❑ Doubles/Doubles Plus One
❑ Tens Partners
❑ Plus Ten

Time
I finished in:

_____

My next goal is:

_____

Name _____   My Score _____

Test Your Skills

7 + 4	3 + 8	10 + 2	11 + 1	4 + 6	12 + 0
5 + 5	3 + 7	7 + 5	8 + 3	5 + 7	10 + 1
2 + 8	4 + 7	9 + 1	7 + 4	6 + 5	11 + 1
12 + 0	4 + 6	8 + 4	6 + 4	5 + 5	4 + 7
5 + 6	6 + 6	1 + 9	11 + 0	10 + 2	4 + 8
7 + 3	11 + 1	8 + 3	10 + 1	7 + 5	9 + 3

How am
I doing?

Accuracy
❏ I got them all right!
❏ I missed a couple.
❏ I will practice these:
(List up to 4 facts.)

Efficiency
I used these strategies:
❏ Count Up +1, +2, +3
❏ Doubles/Doubles Plus One
❏ Tens Partners
❏ Plus Ten

Time
I finished in:

_____

My next goal is:

_____

Name _____   My Score _____

Test Your Skills

13 + 0	8 + 5	9 + 4	10 + 5	6 + 7	14 + 1
13 + 1	12 + 3	9 + 5	15 + 0	11 + 2	10 + 4
8 + 6	4 + 9	11 + 3	12 + 2	11 + 4	12 + 3
10 + 4	12 + 1	14 + 1	15 + 0	10 + 3	13 + 2
12 + 2	10 + 5	11 + 2	5 + 9	13 + 1	8 + 6
9 + 6	13 + 2	8 + 5	7 + 7	4 + 9	7 + 6

How am I doing?

Accuracy
❏ I got them all right!
❏ I missed a couple.
❏ I will practice these:
(List up to 4 facts.)

Efficiency
I used these strategies:
❏ Count Up +1, +2, +3
❏ Doubles/Doubles Plus One
❏ Tens Partners
❏ Plus Ten/Plus Nine

Time
I finished in:

_____

My next goal is:

_____

Name _____   My Score _____

Test Your Skills

8 + 7	6 + 7	5 + 9	10 + 5	13 + 2	7 + 6
8 + 5	14 + 1	15 + 0	6 + 8	9 + 4	11 + 3
7 + 6	10 + 5	11 + 4	13 + 1	8 + 7	7 + 7
9 + 6	13 + 1	12 + 3	8 + 6	11 + 2	10 + 3
5 + 9	14 + 0	12 + 2	5 + 8	12 + 1	13 + 2
9 + 4	6 + 9	9 + 5	7 + 8	15 + 0	12 + 3

How am I doing?

Accuracy
❏ I got them all right!
❏ I missed a couple.
❏ I will practice these:
   (List up to 4 facts.)

Efficiency
I used these strategies:
❏ Count Up +1, +2, +3
❏ Doubles/Doubles Plus One
❏ Tens Partners
❏ Plus Ten/Plus Nine

Time
I finished in:

_____

My next goal is:

_____

Building Math Fluency • EMC 3034 • © Evan-Moor Corp.

Name _____   My Score _____

Test Your Skills

13 + 0	9 + 5	8 + 2	7 + 4	8 + 5	6 + 6
11 + 0	13 + 1	9 + 3	5 + 4	6 + 5	8 + 6
7 + 7	12 + 2	9 + 4	6 + 4	8 + 7	5 + 7
8 + 4	6 + 7	12 + 3	13 + 2	14 + 1	10 + 3
3 + 9	5 + 6	8 + 5	7 + 6	6 + 5	6 + 9
8 + 3	4 + 6	10 + 5	9 + 2	5 + 5	6 + 8

How am I doing?

Accuracy
❏ I got them all right!
❏ I missed a couple.
❏ I will practice these:
(List up to 4 facts.)

Efficiency
I used these strategies:
❏ Count Up +1, +2, +3
❏ Doubles/Doubles Plus One
❏ Tens Partners
❏ Plus Ten/Plus Nine

Time
I finished in:

_____

My next goal is:

_____

Name _____   My Score _____

Test Your Skills

16 + 1	14 + 2	15 + 4	16 + 0	17 + 2	16 + 4
17 + 1	17 + 3	18 + 1	19 + 0	20 + 0	14 + 5
16 + 3	13 + 6	14 + 4	15 + 3	16 + 2	18 + 2
9 + 9	14 + 3	15 + 5	16 + 1	13 + 3	17 + 0
13 + 7	8 + 8	18 + 2	19 + 1	16 + 0	16 + 2
16 + 4	17 + 1	17 + 3	16 + 3	13 + 5	20 + 0

How am I doing?

Accuracy
❏ I got them all right!
❏ I missed a couple.
❏ I will practice these:
(List up to 4 facts.)

Efficiency
I used these strategies:
❏ Count Up +1, +2, +3
❏ Doubles/Doubles Plus One
❏ Tens Partners
❏ Plus Ten/Plus Nine

Time
I finished in:
_____
My next goal is:
_____

Name _____   My Score _____

Test Your Skills

17 + 0	17 + 2	20 + 0	15 + 3	9 + 6	17 + 1
13 + 5	19 + 1	18 + 2	16 + 4	16 + 3	17 + 3
16 + 1	20 + 0	9 + 9	14 + 6	9 + 8	18 + 1
15 + 2	16 + 2	16 + 4	15 + 0	16 + 0	15 + 4
8 + 8	16 + 3	13 + 6	7 + 8	14 + 5	15 + 5
18 + 0	9 + 7	16 + 2	10 + 10	19 + 1	18 + 2

How am I doing?

Accuracy
❑ I got them all right!
❑ I missed a couple.
❑ I will practice these:
(List up to 4 facts.)

Efficiency
I used these strategies:
❑ Count Up +1, +2, +3
❑ Doubles/Doubles Plus One
❑ Tens Partners
❑ Plus Ten/Plus Nine

Time
I finished in:
_____
My next goal is:
_____

Name _____   My Score _____

Test Your Skills

7 + 3	10 + 6	9 + 5	15 + 2	6 + 8	12 + 5
13 + 0	16 + 1	14 + 2	9 + 3	16 + 4	8 + 6
7 + 7	16 + 2	17 + 3	5 + 9	9 + 6	18 + 2
9 + 7	7 + 6	20 + 0	9 + 2	14 + 4	7 + 8
13 + 6	9 + 8	13 + 4	12 + 2	11 + 7	12 + 8
9 + 6	8 + 5	9 + 9	5 + 4	8 + 8	7 + 9

How am I doing?

Accuracy
❏ I got them all right!
❏ I missed a couple.
❏ I will practice these:
(List up to 4 facts.)

Efficiency
I used these strategies:
❏ Count Up +1, +2, +3
❏ Doubles/Doubles Plus One
❏ Tens Partners
❏ Plus Ten/Plus Nine

Time
I finished in:

_____

My next goal is:

_____

Building Math Fluency • EMC 3034 • © Evan-Moor Corp.

Name _____   My Score _____

Test Your Skills

4 − 1	7 − 5	3 − 3	6 − 4	6 − 1	7 − 6
7 − 0	2 − 2	5 − 1	7 − 4	7 − 2	2 − 0
3 − 2	5 − 4	2 − 1	7 − 3	5 − 2	6 − 2
7 − 3	6 − 5	6 − 3	4 − 3	7 − 5	5 − 3
4 − 4	7 − 0	4 − 0	7 − 1	6 − 6	5 − 5
3 − 1	5 − 2	1 − 0	4 − 2	5 − 0	6 − 5

How am I doing?

Accuracy
❑ I got them all right!
❑ I missed a couple.
❑ I will practice these:
(List up to 5 facts.)

Efficiency
I used these strategies:
❑ Count Back −1, −2, −3
❑ Count Up from bottom number
❑ Doubles Subtraction

Time
I finished in:
_____
My next goal is:
_____

Test Your Skills

1 − 0	3 − 1	4 − 2	5 − 0	3 − 0	5 − 5
6 − 3	6 − 5	7 − 3	7 − 5	5 − 3	1 − 1
3 − 3	4 − 1	5 − 2	6 − 1	7 − 7	7 − 6
2 − 1	3 − 2	4 − 3	6 − 6	5 − 4	6 − 2
6 − 4	7 − 2	7 − 4	7 − 6	2 − 2	2 − 0
4 − 0	4 − 4	6 − 0	5 − 2	7 − 5	6 − 5

How am I doing?

Accuracy
❑ I got them all right!
❑ I missed a couple.
❑ I will practice these:
(List up to 5 facts.)

Efficiency
I used these strategies:
❑ Count Back −1, −2, −3
❑ Count Up from bottom number
❑ Doubles Subtraction

Time
I finished in:

_____

My next goal is:

_____

Name _____   My Score _____

Test Your Skills

7 − 2	9 − 2	7 − 6	9 − 6	8 − 2	9 − 7
8 − 6	7 − 4	9 − 4	8 − 0	9 − 8	10 − 1
10 − 2	7 − 3	10 − 6	7 − 7	8 − 3	8 − 8
9 − 3	10 − 4	7 − 5	10 − 8	8 − 1	10 − 10
8 − 5	10 − 5	9 − 3	10 − 9	9 − 9	10 − 0
10 − 3	8 − 7	10 − 7	9 − 5	9 − 1	8 − 4

How am I doing?

Accuracy
❏ I got them all right!
❏ I missed a couple.
❏ I will practice these:
(List up to 5 facts.)

Efficiency
I used these strategies:
❏ Count Back −1, −2, −3
❏ Count Up from bottom number
❏ Doubles Subtraction
❏ Tens Partners Subtraction

Time
I finished in:
_____

My next goal is:
_____

Name _____   My Score _____

Test Your Skills

$$9 - 3$$ $$10 - 0$$ $$8 - 5$$ $$9 - 5$$ $$10 - 4$$ $$9 - 7$$

$$10 - 6$$ $$8 - 8$$ $$7 - 2$$ $$10 - 8$$ $$8 - 7$$ $$10 - 10$$

$$10 - 7$$ $$9 - 9$$ $$10 - 3$$ $$9 - 6$$ $$10 - 5$$ $$9 - 1$$

$$9 - 4$$ $$10 - 1$$ $$8 - 6$$ $$10 - 9$$ $$9 - 2$$ $$9 - 8$$

$$7 - 6$$ $$8 - 4$$ $$10 - 2$$ $$8 - 0$$ $$7 - 4$$ $$8 - 2$$

$$7 - 5$$ $$8 - 3$$ $$9 - 7$$ $$7 - 7$$ $$7 - 3$$ $$8 - 1$$

How am I doing?

Accuracy
❏ I got them all right!
❏ I missed a couple.
❏ I will practice these:
   (List up to 5 facts.)

Efficiency
I used these strategies:
❏ Count Back −1, −2, −3
❏ Count Up from bottom number
❏ Doubles Subtraction
❏ Tens Partners Subtraction

Time
I finished in:

_____

My next goal is:

_____

Building Math Fluency • EMC 3034 • © Evan-Moor Corp.

Name _____   My Score _____

Test Your Skills

5 − 2	7 − 3	9 − 4	10 − 5	8 − 6	7 − 7
6 − 5	9 − 2	8 − 3	6 − 2	8 − 5	7 − 4
8 − 7	10 − 3	8 − 4	7 − 5	10 − 6	8 − 2
10 − 1	9 − 3	10 − 4	9 − 6	10 − 8	5 − 1
10 − 10	8 − 0	6 − 3	10 − 7	5 − 3	10 − 9
4 − 2	6 − 4	7 − 2	9 − 1	9 − 5	5 − 4

How am I doing?

Accuracy
❏ I got them all right!
❏ I missed a couple.
❏ I will practice these:
(List up to 5 facts.)

Efficiency
I used these strategies:
❏ Count Back −1, −2, −3
❏ Count Up from bottom number
❏ Doubles Subtraction
❏ Tens Partners Subtraction

Time
I finished in:

_____

My next goal is:

_____

Name _____   My Score _____

Test Your Skills

10 − 0	11 − 8	12 − 4	10 − 6	11 − 7	10 − 9
11 − 2	10 − 5	11 − 6	10 − 2	12 − 3	11 − 10
11 − 5	10 − 7	12 − 9	11 − 1	12 − 1	11 − 4
12 − 3	10 − 1	11 − 9	12 − 7	10 − 8	10 − 10
10 − 4	12 − 4	12 − 5	10 − 3	12 − 2	11 − 8
12 − 6	12 − 8	10 − 10	12 − 0	11 − 4	12 − 7

How am I doing?

Accuracy
❏ I got them all right!
❏ I missed a couple.
❏ I will practice these:
(List up to 4 facts.)

Efficiency
I used these strategies:
❏ Count Back/Count Up
❏ Think Addition
❏ Other:

Time
I finished in:
_____
My next goal is:
_____

Name _____   My Score _____

Test Your Skills

12 − 7	11 − 1	10 − 7	12 − 5	11 − 9	12 − 1
11 − 5	10 − 10	12 − 4	11 − 3	10 − 3	12 − 2
10 − 1	12 − 9	11 − 2	12 − 3	11 − 7	10 − 8
11 − 4	11 − 8	10 − 9	11 − 5	10 − 6	11 − 10
12 − 8	12 − 0	10 − 2	12 − 6	12 − 7	11 − 4
11 − 8	10 − 6	12 − 4	11 − 9	10 − 4	11 − 10

How am
I doing?

Accuracy
❏ I got them all right!
❏ I missed a couple.
❏ I will practice these:
  (List up to 4 facts.)

Efficiency
I used these strategies:
❏ Count Back/Count Up
❏ Think Addition
❏ Other:

Time
I finished in:
_____

My next goal is:
_____

Name _____   My Score _____

Test Your Skills

14 − 8	14 − 4	15 − 8	14 − 6	13 − 10	14 − 5
13 − 2	14 − 9	15 − 4	13 − 6	15 − 10	15 − 1
14 − 2	13 − 0	14 − 1	13 − 7	15 − 2	14 − 6
14 − 10	13 − 5	15 − 0	13 − 9	14 − 9	13 − 4
13 − 3	14 − 8	15 − 5	14 − 7	15 − 9	14 − 3
13 − 7	15 − 3	13 − 0	15 − 8	13 − 1	15 − 6

How am I doing?

Accuracy
❑ I got them all right!
❑ I missed a couple.
❑ I will practice these:
(List up to 4 facts.)

Efficiency
I used these strategies:
❑ Count Back/Count Up
❑ Think Addition
❑ Minus Ten/Minus Nine
❑ Other:

Time
I finished in:
_____
My next goal is:
_____

Name _____   My Score _____

Test Your Skills

15 − 4	15 − 8	14 − 9	14 − 7	13 − 7	15 − 6
15 − 1	14 − 4	13 − 5	13 − 3	14 − 6	13 − 9
13 − 6	14 − 0	13 − 4	13 − 1	14 − 5	13 − 8
15 − 5	15 − 9	14 − 2	14 − 8	14 − 3	15 − 7
15 − 3	13 − 6	13 − 0	13 − 8	15 − 6	15 − 15
14 − 1	15 − 0	14 − 8	13 − 2	14 − 9	15 − 2

How am I doing?

Accuracy
❏ I got them all right!
❏ I missed a couple.
❏ I will practice these:
(List up to 4 facts.)

Efficiency
I used these strategies:
❏ Count Back/Count Up
❏ Think Addition
❏ Minus Ten/Minus Nine
❏ Other:

Time
I finished in:
_____

My next goal is:
_____

Name _____   My Score _____

Test Your Skills

13 − 10	14 − 6	13 − 8	14 − 4	10 − 9	14 − 5
15 − 8	10 − 3	13 − 9	12 − 6	15 − 7	11 − 8
8 − 3	7 − 5	15 − 2	9 − 7	8 − 5	7 − 3
13 − 4	12 − 3	13 − 5	11 − 2	12 − 7	15 − 6
14 − 9	15 − 5	9 − 8	10 − 7	14 − 8	15 − 10
10 − 4	9 − 6	15 − 4	14 − 2	10 − 8	9 − 5

How am I doing?

Accuracy
❏ I got them all right!
❏ I missed a couple.
❏ I will practice these:
  (List up to 4 facts.)

Efficiency
I used these strategies:
❏ Count Back/Count Up
❏ Think Addition
❏ Minus Ten/Minus Nine
❏ Other:

Time
I finished in:
_____

My next goal is:
_____

Name _____   My Score _____

Test Your Skills

17 − 4	16 − 6	15 − 8	17 − 8	16 − 5	17 − 7
16 − 9	15 − 4	17 − 6	15 − 10	17 − 9	15 − 2
16 − 3	17 − 3	16 − 0	15 − 5	16 − 9	15 − 9
16 − 4	15 − 15	16 − 8	15 − 7	17 − 5	15 − 8
17 − 9	15 − 0	15 − 3	16 − 7	17 − 2	17 − 7
16 − 10	17 − 5	15 − 6	17 − 1	15 − 4	16 − 2

How am I doing?

Accuracy
❏ I got them all right!
❏ I missed a couple.
❏ I will practice these:
(List up to 4 facts.)

Efficiency
I used these strategies:
❏ Count Back/Count Up
❏ Think Addition
❏ Minus Ten/Minus Nine
❏ Other:

Time
I finished in:
_____

My next goal is:
_____

Test Your Skills

16 − 0	15 − 7	16 − 3	15 − 9	17 − 3	15 − 5
16 − 8	17 − 4	16 − 4	17 − 7	15 − 6	17 − 5
16 − 5	16 − 9	15 − 4	16 − 7	16 − 6	15 − 15
14 − 9	15 − 10	16 − 2	17 − 3	15 − 4	16 − 8
17 − 6	17 − 9	16 − 9	15 − 2	16 − 4	17 − 8
15 − 3	17 − 2	15 − 8	17 − 1	17 − 10	16 − 7

How am I doing?

Accuracy
❏ I got them all right!
❏ I missed a couple.
❏ I will practice these:
  (List up to 4 facts.)

Efficiency
I used these strategies:
❏ Count Back/Count Up
❏ Think Addition
❏ Minus Ten/Minus Nine
❏ Other:

Time
I finished in:
_____

My next goal is:
_____

Name _____   My Score _____

Test Your Skills

18 − 4	18 − 6	19 − 8	20 − 6	19 − 5	20 − 20
19 − 9	20 − 7	20 − 4	18 − 10	20 − 8	19 − 7
18 − 2	19 − 3	19 − 1	20 − 2	18 − 5	19 − 4
18 − 5	20 − 1	19 − 10	18 − 9	20 − 9	19 − 8
19 − 10	18 − 7	20 − 5	20 − 7	19 − 6	18 − 3
18 − 0	19 − 2	20 − 3	19 − 4	18 − 10	20 − 0

How am I doing?

Accuracy
❑ I got them all right!
❑ I missed a couple.
❑ I will practice these:
   (List up to 4 facts.)

Efficiency
I used these strategies:
❑ Count Back/Count Up
❑ Think Addition
❑ Minus Ten/Minus Nine
❑ Other:

Time
I finished in:
_____
My next goal is:
_____

Name _____   My Score _____

Test Your Skills

19 − 3	18 − 1	20 − 8	18 − 2	19 − 6	19 − 1
20 − 1	20 − 9	19 − 10	20 − 4	18 − 3	20 − 5
18 − 0	20 − 2	20 − 6	19 − 9	20 − 10	18 − 4
18 − 6	19 − 5	18 − 10	20 − 3	19 − 7	18 − 8
19 − 2	18 − 5	19 − 0	18 − 1	20 − 7	20 − 4
18 − 7	19 − 6	19 − 4	18 − 3	19 − 8	18 − 9

How am I doing?

Accuracy
❏ I got them all right!
❏ I missed a couple.
❏ I will practice these:
(List up to 4 facts.)

Efficiency
I used these strategies:
❏ Count Back/Count Up
❏ Think Addition
❏ Minus Ten/Minus Nine
❏ Other:

Time
I finished in:
_____

My next goal is:
_____

Test Your Skills

18 − 4	20 − 9	18 − 7	19 − 4	18 − 10	19 − 5
19 − 9	20 − 8	19 − 7	20 − 0	17 − 6	20 − 5
20 − 6	16 − 9	17 − 9	20 − 10	18 − 2	19 − 3
19 − 2	15 − 6	18 − 1	18 − 5	20 − 3	20 − 1
17 − 8	16 − 5	12 − 6	15 − 7	18 − 8	14 − 6
14 − 9	13 − 8	16 − 8	14 − 8	15 − 4	20 − 2

How am I doing?

Accuracy
❏ I got them all right!
❏ I missed a couple.
❏ I will practice these:
(List up to 4 facts.)

Efficiency
I used these strategies:
❏ Count Back/Count Up
❏ Think Addition
❏ Minus Ten/Minus Nine
❏ Other

Time
I finished in:
_____

My next goal is:
_____

How to Use
Facts Flashcards

Practice with flashcards can help students gain automaticity with math facts. Flashcards enable students to work at their own pace and to focus on the specific facts that they need to learn.

Prepare the Flashcards

- Reproduce the cards that students need to practice. Within each operation, the cards progress from easier to more difficult facts. Keep the cards to a manageable number; add new cards as facts are mastered.

- Students cut the cards apart and store them in an envelope or a self-sealing plastic bag.

1+1	2+0	2+1	2+2
Addition	Addition	Addition	Addition
3+0	3+1	3+2	3+3
Addition	Addition	Addition	Addition
4+1	4+2	4+3	4+4
Addition			Addition

Tips for Practicing the Flashcards

- When students practice independently, encourage them to softly say the facts aloud to incorporate the aural modality.

- Have students practice with a partner. This is more fun and it ensures that students are computing each answer and not just looking at the answer.
If an answer is incorrect, the partner should say, for example, "No, 8 + 6 is 14." Then the answering student should repeat the equation aloud.

- Have students sort and then practice the cards by the strategies they would use to compute the answers. For example:

    Easy Facts—Plus Zero or Minus Zero; Count Up +1, +2, +3
    Doubles Addition or Doubles Subtraction
    Doubles Plus One
    Tens Partners
    Count Back or Count Up Subtraction

- Allow students to personalize their cards to show the strategies used to compute the answers.

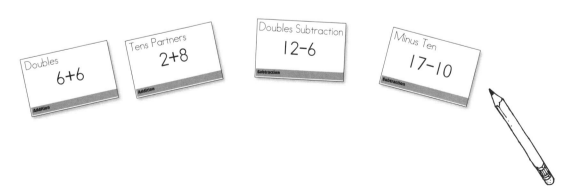

Building Math Fluency • EMC 3034 • © Evan-Moor Corp.

$2 + 2$	$2 + 1$	$2 + 0$	$1 + 1$
Addition	Addition	Addition	Addition
$3 + 3$	$3 + 2$	$3 + 1$	$3 + 0$
Addition	Addition	Addition	Addition
$4 + 4$	$4 + 3$	$4 + 2$	$4 + 1$
Addition	Addition	Addition	Addition

4

Building Math Fluency
EMC 3034 • © Evan-Moor Corp.

3

Building Math Fluency
EMC 3034 • © Evan-Moor Corp.

2

Building Math Fluency
EMC 3034 • © Evan-Moor Corp.

6

Building Math Fluency
EMC 3034 • © Evan-Moor Corp.

5

Building Math Fluency
EMC 3034 • © Evan-Moor Corp.

4

Building Math Fluency
EMC 3034 • © Evan-Moor Corp.

2

Building Math Fluency
EMC 3034 • © Evan-Moor Corp.

8

Building Math Fluency
EMC 3034 • © Evan-Moor Corp.

7

Building Math Fluency
EMC 3034 • © Evan-Moor Corp.

6

Building Math Fluency
EMC 3034 • © Evan-Moor Corp.

5

Building Math Fluency
EMC 3034 • © Evan-Moor Corp.

$5 + 0$	$5 + 1$	$5 + 2$	$5 + 3$
Addition	Addition	Addition	Addition
$5 + 4$	$5 + 5$	$6 + 0$	$6 + 1$
Addition	Addition	Addition	Addition
$6 + 2$	$6 + 3$	$6 + 4$	$6 + 5$
Addition	Addition	Addition	Addition

8

7

6

11

10

6

10

5

8

9

9

7 + 2	7 + 1	7 + 0	6 + 6
Addition	Addition	Addition	Addition
7 + 6	7 + 5	7 + 4	7 + 3
Addition	Addition	Addition	Addition
8 + 2	8 + 1	8 + 0	7 + 7
Addition	Addition	Addition	Addition

9

8

7

12

13

12

11

10

10

9

8

14

$8 + 6$	Addition	$9 + 1$	Addition	$9 + 5$	Addition
$8 + 5$	Addition	$9 + 0$	Addition	$9 + 4$	Addition
$8 + 4$	Addition	$8 + 8$	Addition	$9 + 3$	Addition
$8 + 3$	Addition	$8 + 7$	Addition	$9 + 2$	Addition

14	13	12	11
Building Math Fluency EMC 3034 • © Evan-Moor Corp.	Building Math Fluency EMC 3034 • © Evan-Moor Corp.	Building Math Fluency EMC 3034 • © Evan-Moor Corp.	Building Math Fluency EMC 3034 • © Evan-Moor Corp.
10	9	16	15
Building Math Fluency EMC 3034 • © Evan-Moor Corp.	Building Math Fluency EMC 3034 • © Evan-Moor Corp.	Building Math Fluency EMC 3034 • © Evan-Moor Corp.	Building Math Fluency EMC 3034 • © Evan-Moor Corp.
14	13	12	11
Building Math Fluency EMC 3034 • © Evan-Moor Corp.	Building Math Fluency EMC 3034 • © Evan-Moor Corp.	Building Math Fluency EMC 3034 • © Evan-Moor Corp.	Building Math Fluency EMC 3034 • © Evan-Moor Corp.

$9 + 9$		$10 + 3$		$10 + 7$
	Addition		Addition		Addition
$9 + 8$		$10 + 2$		$10 + 6$
	Addition		Addition		Addition
$9 + 7$		$10 + 1$		$10 + 5$
	Addition		Addition		Addition
$9 + 6$		$10 + 0$		$10 + 4$
	Addition		Addition		Addition

18

Building Math Fluency
EMC 3034 • © Evan-Moor Corp.

17

Building Math Fluency
EMC 3034 • © Evan-Moor Corp.

16

Building Math Fluency
EMC 3034 • © Evan-Moor Corp.

15

Building Math Fluency
EMC 3034 • © Evan-Moor Corp.

13

Building Math Fluency
EMC 3034 • © Evan-Moor Corp.

12

Building Math Fluency
EMC 3034 • © Evan-Moor Corp.

11

Building Math Fluency
EMC 3034 • © Evan-Moor Corp.

10

Building Math Fluency
EMC 3034 • © Evan-Moor Corp.

17

Building Math Fluency
EMC 3034 • © Evan-Moor Corp.

16

Building Math Fluency
EMC 3034 • © Evan-Moor Corp.

15

Building Math Fluency
EMC 3034 • © Evan-Moor Corp.

14

Building Math Fluency
EMC 3034 • © Evan-Moor Corp.

$11+0$	$11+4$	$11+8$
Addition	Addition	Addition
$10+10$	$11+3$	$11+7$
Addition	Addition	Addition
$10+9$	$11+2$	$11+6$
Addition	Addition	Addition
$10+8$	$11+1$	$11+5$
Addition	Addition	Addition

11

20

19

18

15

14

13

12

19

18

17

16

$12 + 2$	$12 + 1$	$12 + 0$	$11 + 9$
Addition		Addition	
$12 + 6$	$12 + 5$	$12 + 4$	$12 + 3$
Addition		Addition	
$13 + 1$	$13 + 0$	$12 + 8$	$12 + 7$
Addition		Addition	

14

13

12

18

17

16

14

13

20

20

15

19

$13 + 5$	$14 + 1$	$14 + 5$
Addition	Addition	Addition
$13 + 4$	$14 + 0$	$14 + 4$
Addition	Addition	Addition
$13 + 3$	$13 + 7$	$14 + 3$
Addition	Addition	Addition
$13 + 2$	$13 + 6$	$14 + 2$
Addition	Addition	Addition

18

17

16

15

15

14

20

19

19

18

17

16

$15 + 2$	$16 + 0$	$16 + 4$
Addition	Addition	Addition
$15 + 1$	$15 + 5$	$16 + 3$
Addition	Addition	Addition
$15 + 0$	$15 + 4$	$16 + 2$
Addition	Addition	Addition
$14 + 6$	$15 + 3$	$16 + 1$
Addition	Addition	Addition

17

16

15

16

20

19

20

19

18

18

17

18 + 0

Addition

19 + 1

Addition

17 + 2

Addition

19 + 0

Addition

17 + 1

Addition

18 + 2

Addition

17 + 0

Addition

18 + 1

Addition

20 + 0

Addition

18

19

18

17

20

19

20

19

20

8 − 0	7 − 1	5 − 2
Subtraction	Subtraction	Subtraction
5 − 0	3 − 1	4 − 2
Subtraction	Subtraction	Subtraction
4 − 0	2 − 1	3 − 2
Subtraction	Subtraction	Subtraction
1 − 0	10 − 0	10 − 1
Subtraction	Subtraction	Subtraction

8

6

3

5

2

2

4

1

10

1

1

9

9 − 2	8 − 2	7 − 2	6 − 2
Subtraction	Subtraction	Subtraction	Subtraction
5 − 3	4 − 3	3 − 3	10 − 2
Subtraction	Subtraction	Subtraction	Subtraction
9 − 3	8 − 3	7 − 3	6 − 3
Subtraction	Subtraction	Subtraction	Subtraction

7

Building Math Fluency
EMC 3034 • © Evan-Moor Corp.

6

Building Math Fluency
EMC 3034 • © Evan-Moor Corp.

5

Building Math Fluency
EMC 3034 • © Evan-Moor Corp.

4

Building Math Fluency
EMC 3034 • © Evan-Moor Corp.

2

Building Math Fluency
EMC 3034 • © Evan-Moor Corp.

1

Building Math Fluency
EMC 3034 • © Evan-Moor Corp.

0

Building Math Fluency
EMC 3034 • © Evan-Moor Corp.

8

Building Math Fluency
EMC 3034 • © Evan-Moor Corp.

6

Building Math Fluency
EMC 3034 • © Evan-Moor Corp.

5

Building Math Fluency
EMC 3034 • © Evan-Moor Corp.

4

Building Math Fluency
EMC 3034 • © Evan-Moor Corp.

3

Building Math Fluency
EMC 3034 • © Evan-Moor Corp.

	Subtraction		Subtraction
$7 - 4$		$5 - 5$	
$6 - 4$	Subtraction	$10 - 4$	Subtraction
$5 - 4$		$9 - 4$	Subtraction
$10 - 3$	Subtraction	$8 - 4$	Subtraction

	Subtraction
$9 - 5$	
$8 - 5$	Subtraction
$7 - 5$	Subtraction
$6 - 5$	Subtraction

3

2

1

0

6

5

4

3

2

1

4

7

9 − 6	10 − 7	10 − 10
Subtraction	Subtraction	Subtraction
8 − 6	9 − 7	10 − 9
Subtraction	Subtraction	Subtraction
7 − 6	8 − 7	10 − 8
Subtraction	Subtraction	Subtraction
10 − 5	10 − 6	9 − 8
Subtraction	Subtraction	Subtraction

3

2

1

5

3

2

1

4

0

1

2

1

$12 - 2$	$13 - 4$	$17 - 4$
Subtraction	Subtraction	Subtraction
$11 - 2$	$12 - 4$	$16 - 4$
Subtraction	Subtraction	Subtraction
$20 - 1$	$11 - 4$	$15 - 4$
Subtraction	Subtraction	Subtraction
$20 - 0$	$13 - 2$	$14 - 4$
Subtraction	Subtraction	Subtraction

Building Math Fluency
EMC 3034 • © Evan-Moor Corp.

10

Building Math Fluency
EMC 3034 • © Evan-Moor Corp.

9

Building Math Fluency
EMC 3034 • © Evan-Moor Corp.

13

Building Math Fluency
EMC 3034 • © Evan-Moor Corp.

9

Building Math Fluency
EMC 3034 • © Evan-Moor Corp.

8

Building Math Fluency
EMC 3034 • © Evan-Moor Corp.

12

Building Math Fluency
EMC 3034 • © Evan-Moor Corp.

19

Building Math Fluency
EMC 3034 • © Evan-Moor Corp.

7

Building Math Fluency
EMC 3034 • © Evan-Moor Corp.

11

Building Math Fluency
EMC 3034 • © Evan-Moor Corp.

20

Building Math Fluency
EMC 3034 • © Evan-Moor Corp.

11

Building Math Fluency
EMC 3034 • © Evan-Moor Corp.

10

11 − 5	20 − 4	19 − 4	18 − 4
Subtraction	Subtraction	Subtraction	Subtraction
15 − 5	14 − 5	13 − 5	12 − 5
Subtraction	Subtraction	Subtraction	Subtraction
19 − 5	18 − 5	17 − 5	16 − 5
Subtraction	Subtraction	Subtraction	Subtraction

6	16	15	14
Building Math Fluency EMC 3034 • © Evan-Moor Corp.	Building Math Fluency EMC 3034 • © Evan-Moor Corp.	Building Math Fluency EMC 3034 • © Evan-Moor Corp.	Building Math Fluency EMC 3034 • © Evan-Moor Corp.
10	9	8	7
Building Math Fluency EMC 3034 • © Evan-Moor Corp.	Building Math Fluency EMC 3034 • © Evan-Moor Corp.	Building Math Fluency EMC 3034 • © Evan-Moor Corp.	Building Math Fluency EMC 3034 • © Evan-Moor Corp.
14	13	12	11
Building Math Fluency EMC 3034 • © Evan-Moor Corp.	Building Math Fluency EMC 3034 • © Evan-Moor Corp.	Building Math Fluency EMC 3034 • © Evan-Moor Corp.	Building Math Fluency EMC 3034 • © Evan-Moor Corp.

$13 - 6$	$12 - 6$	$11 - 6$	$20 - 5$
Subtraction	Subtraction	Subtraction	Subtraction
$17 - 6$	$16 - 6$	$15 - 6$	$14 - 6$
Subtraction	Subtraction	Subtraction	Subtraction
$11 - 7$	$20 - 6$	$19 - 6$	$18 - 6$
Subtraction	Subtraction	Subtraction	Subtraction

7

Building Math Fluency
EMC 3034 • © Evan-Moor Corp.

6

Building Math Fluency
EMC 3034 • © Evan-Moor Corp.

5

Building Math Fluency
EMC 3034 • © Evan-Moor Corp.

11

Building Math Fluency
EMC 3034 • © Evan-Moor Corp.

10

Building Math Fluency
EMC 3034 • © Evan-Moor Corp.

15

Building Math Fluency
EMC 3034 • © Evan-Moor Corp.

4

Building Math Fluency
EMC 3034 • © Evan-Moor Corp.

14

Building Math Fluency
EMC 3034 • © Evan-Moor Corp.

13

Building Math Fluency
EMC 3034 • © Evan-Moor Corp.

9

Building Math Fluency
EMC 3034 • © Evan-Moor Corp.

8

Building Math Fluency
EMC 3034 • © Evan-Moor Corp.

12

Building Math Fluency
EMC 3034 • © Evan-Moor Corp.

$15 - 7$	$14 - 7$	$13 - 7$	$12 - 7$
Subtraction	Subtraction	Subtraction	Subtraction
$19 - 7$	$18 - 7$	$17 - 7$	$16 - 7$
Subtraction	Subtraction	Subtraction	Subtraction
$13 - 8$	$12 - 8$	$11 - 8$	$20 - 7$
Subtraction	Subtraction	Subtraction	Subtraction

8

7

6

5

12

11

10

9

5

4

3

13

$17 - 8$	Subtraction	$11 - 9$	Subtraction	$15 - 9$	Subtraction
$16 - 8$	Subtraction	$20 - 8$	Subtraction	$14 - 9$	Subtraction
$15 - 8$	Subtraction	$19 - 8$	Subtraction	$13 - 9$	Subtraction
$14 - 8$	Subtraction	$18 - 8$	Subtraction	$12 - 9$	Subtraction

9

Building Math Fluency
EMC 3034 • © Evan-Moor Corp.

8

Building Math Fluency
EMC 3034 • © Evan-Moor Corp.

7

Building Math Fluency
EMC 3034 • © Evan-Moor Corp.

6

Building Math Fluency
EMC 3034 • © Evan-Moor Corp.

2

Building Math Fluency
EMC 3034 • © Evan-Moor Corp.

12

Building Math Fluency
EMC 3034 • © Evan-Moor Corp.

11

Building Math Fluency
EMC 3034 • © Evan-Moor Corp.

10

Building Math Fluency
EMC 3034 • © Evan-Moor Corp.

6

Building Math Fluency
EMC 3034 • © Evan-Moor Corp.

5

Building Math Fluency
EMC 3034 • © Evan-Moor Corp.

4

Building Math Fluency
EMC 3034 • © Evan-Moor Corp.

3

Building Math Fluency
EMC 3034 • © Evan-Moor Corp.

146

Building Math Fluency • EMC 3034 • © Evan-Moor Corp.

	Subtraction		Subtraction		Subtraction
$19 - 9$		$13 - 10$		$17 - 10$	
$18 - 9$	Subtraction	$12 - 10$	Subtraction	$16 - 10$	Subtraction
$17 - 9$	Subtraction	$11 - 10$	Subtraction	$15 - 10$	Subtraction
$16 - 9$	Subtraction	$20 - 9$	Subtraction	$14 - 10$	Subtraction

10

9

8

7

3

2

1

11

7

6

5

4

Answer Key

Page 8

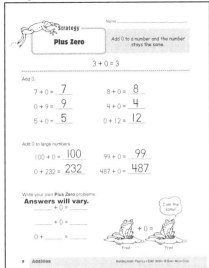

Strategy — Plus Zero — Add 0 to a number and the number stays the same.

3 + 0 = 3

Add 0.

7 + 0 = **7**   8 + 0 = **8**
0 + 9 = **9**   4 + 0 = **4**
5 + 0 = **5**   0 + 12 = **12**

Add 0 to large numbers.

100 + 0 = **100**   99 + 0 = **99**
0 + 232 = **232**   487 + 0 = **487**

Write your own Plus Zero problems.
Answers will vary.

____ + 0 = ____

____ + 0 = ____

0 + ____ = ____

Page 9

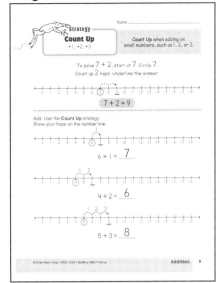

Strategy — Count Up +1, +2, +3 — Count Up when adding on small numbers, such as 1, 2, or 3.

To solve 7 + 2, start at 7. Circle 7.
Count up 2 hops. Underline the answer.

7 + 2 = 9

Add. Use the Count Up strategy.
Show your hops on the number line.

6 + 1 = **7**

4 + 2 = **6**

5 + 3 = **8**

Page 10

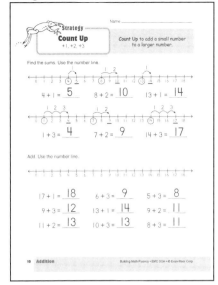

Strategy — Count Up +1, +2, +3 — Count Up to add a small number to a larger number.

Find the sums. Use the number line.

4 + 1 = **5**   8 + 2 = **10**   13 + 1 = **14**

1 + 3 = **4**   7 + 2 = **9**   14 + 3 = **17**

Add. Use the number line.

17 + 1 = **18**   6 + 3 = **9**   5 + 3 = **8**
9 + 3 = **12**   13 + 1 = **14**   9 + 2 = **11**
11 + 2 = **13**   10 + 3 = **13**   8 + 3 = **11**

Page 11

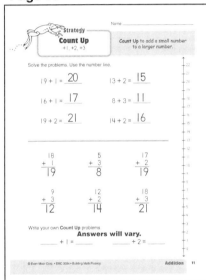

Strategy — Count Up +1, +2, +3 — Count Up to add a small number to a larger number.

Solve the problems. Use the number line.

19 + 1 = **20**   13 + 2 = **15**
16 + 1 = **17**   8 + 3 = **11**
19 + 2 = **21**   14 + 2 = **16**

18 + 1 = **19**   5 + 3 = **8**   17 + 2 = **19**

9 + 3 = **12**   12 + 2 = **14**   18 + 3 = **21**

Write your own Count Up problems.
Answers will vary.

____ + 1 = ____   ____ + 2 = ____

Page 12

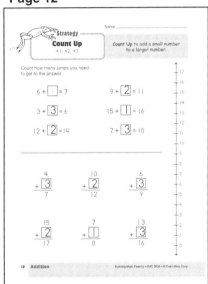

Strategy — Count Up +1, +2, +3 — Count Up to add a small number to a larger number.

Count how many jumps you need to get to the answer.

6 + **1** = 7   9 + **2** = 11
3 + **3** = 6   15 + **1** = 16
12 + **2** = 14   7 + **3** = 10

4 + **3** = 7   10 + **2** = 12   6 + **3** = 9

15 + **2** = 17   7 + **1** = 8   13 + **3** = 16

Page 13

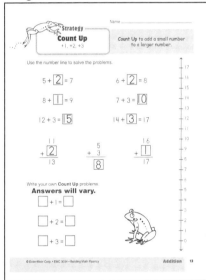

Strategy — Count Up +1, +2, +3 — Count Up to add a small number to a larger number.

Use the number line to solve the problems.

5 + **2** = 7   6 + **2** = 8
8 + **1** = 9   7 + 3 = **10**
12 + 3 = **15**   14 + **3** = 17

11 + **2** = 13   5 + 3 = **8**   16 + **1** = 17

Write your own Count Up problems.
Answers will vary.

____ + 1 = ____

____ + 2 = ____

____ + 3 = ____

Page 14

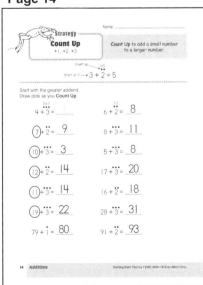

Strategy — Count Up +1, +2, +3 — Count Up to add a small number to a larger number.

Start at 3 → 3 + 2 = 5

Start with the greater addend.
Draw dots as you Count Up.

4 + 3 = **7**   6 + 2 = **8**
7 + 2 = **9**   8 + 3 = **11**
10 + 3 = **13**   5 + 3 = **8**
12 + 2 = **14**   17 + 3 = **20**
11 + 3 = **14**   16 + 2 = **18**
19 + 3 = **22**   28 + 3 = **31**
79 + 1 = **80**   91 + 2 = **93**

Page 15

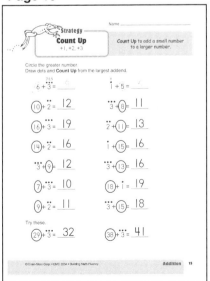

Strategy — Count Up +1, +2, +3 — Count Up to add a small number to a larger number.

Circle the greater number.
Draw dots and Count Up from the largest addend.

6 + 3 =   1 + 5 =

10 + 2 = **12**   3 + 8 = **11**
16 + 3 = **19**   2 + 11 = **13**
14 + 2 = **16**   1 + 15 = **16**
3 + 9 = **12**   3 + 13 = **16**
7 + 3 = **10**   18 + 1 = **19**
9 + 2 = **11**   3 + 15 = **18**

Try these.

29 + 3 = **32**   38 + 3 = **41**

Page 16

Strategy — Count Up +1, +2, +3 — Count Up to add a small number to a larger number.

Solve the problems.

15 + 2 = **17**   17 + 3 = **20**   21 + 2 = **23**
                    16 + 2 = **18**
18 + 3 = **21**   19 + 2 = **21**
3 + 10 = **13**   3 + 11 = **14**   15 + 3 = **18**

Think about how you solved the problems. Mark yes or no.
Answers will vary.

Did you:		yes	no
draw dots to count up?	19 + 2	☐	☐
count up from the larger number?	19 + 2	☐	☐
use a number line?		☐	☐

Page 17

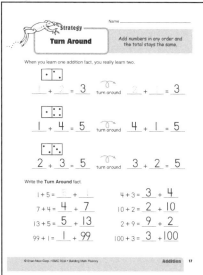

Page 18

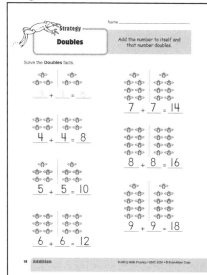

Page 19

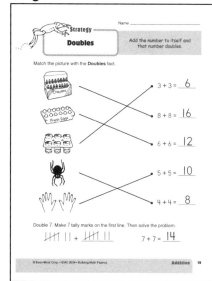

Page 20

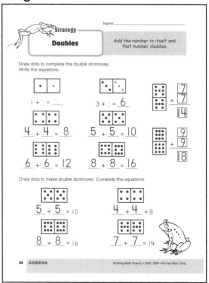

Page 21

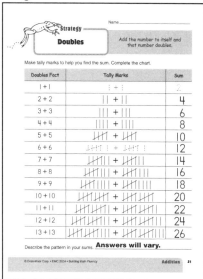

Page 22

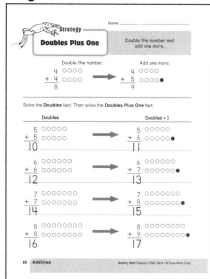

Page 23

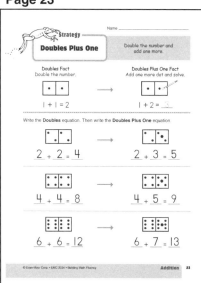

Page 24

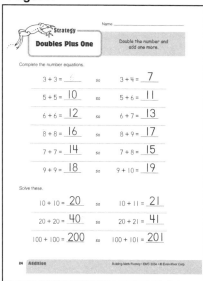

Page 25

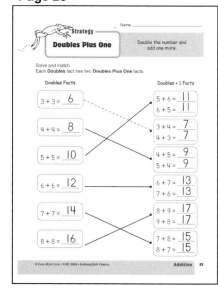

Page 26

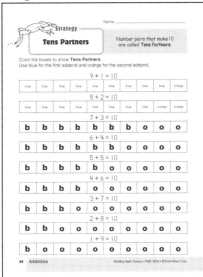

Page 27

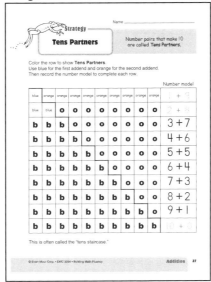

Page 28

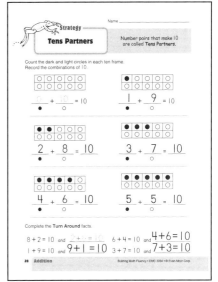

Page 29

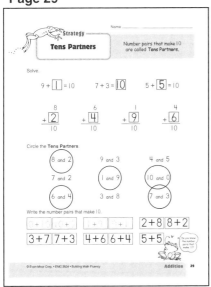

Page 30

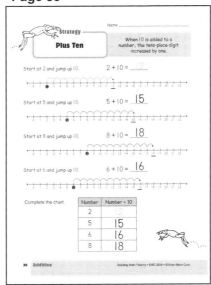

Page 31

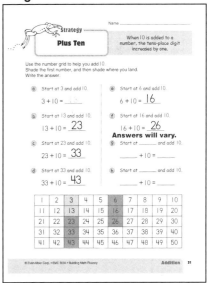

Page 32

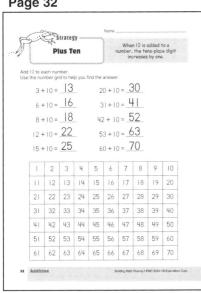

Page 33

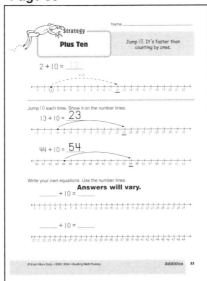

Page 34

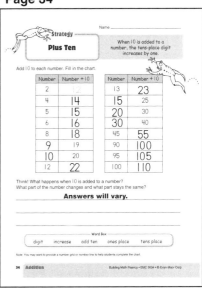

Page 35

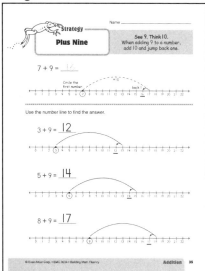

Page 36

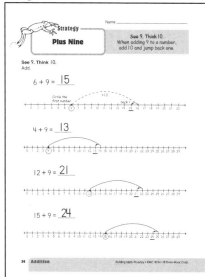

Page 37

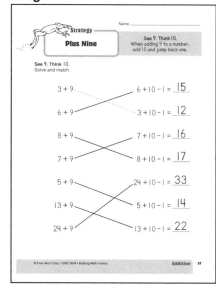

Page 38

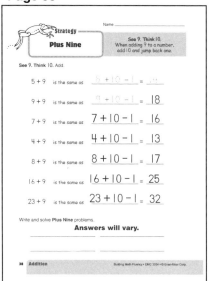

Page 39

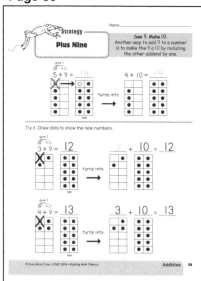

Page 40

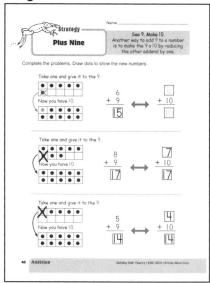

Page 41

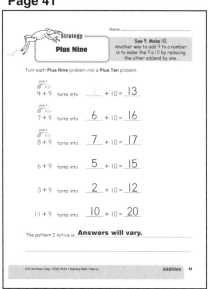

Page 42

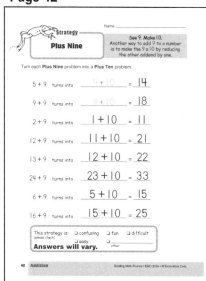

Page 43

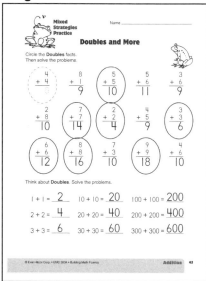

Page 44

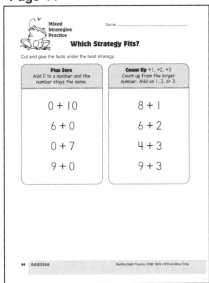

Page 45

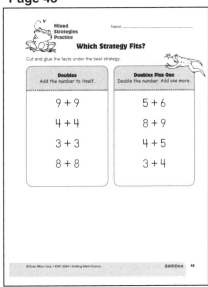

Page 46

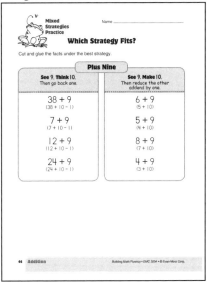

Page 47

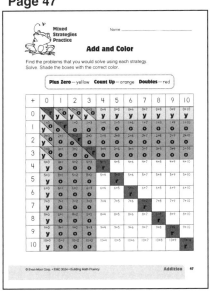

Page 48

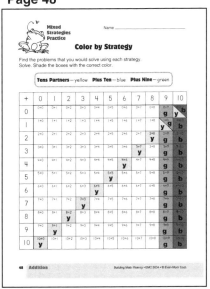

Page 49

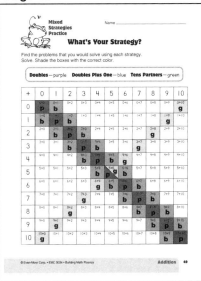

Page 50

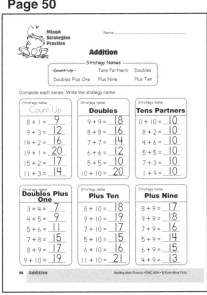

Page 51

Page 54

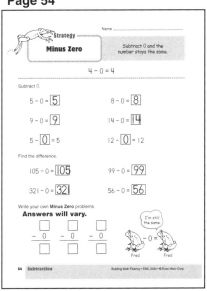

Page 55

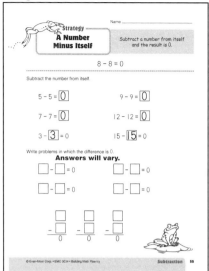

Page 56

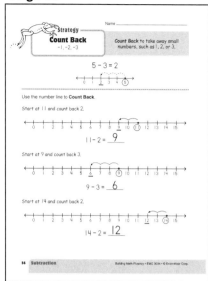

Page 57

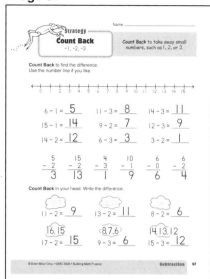

Page 58

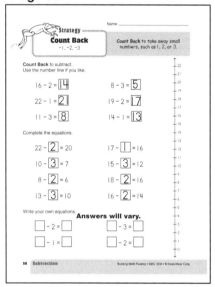

Page 59

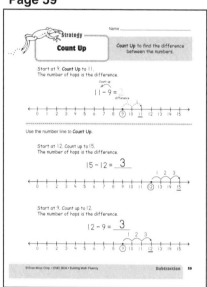

Page 60

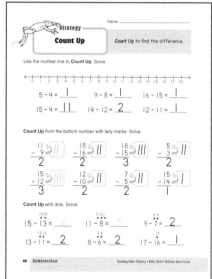

Page 61

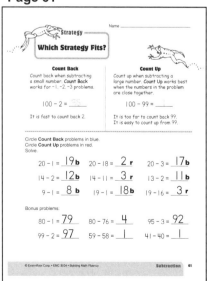

Page 62

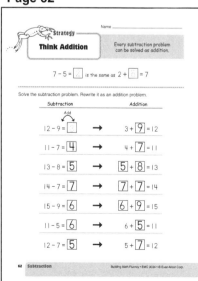

Page 63

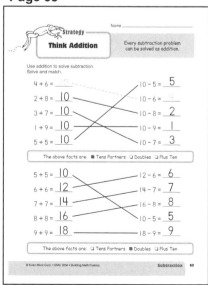

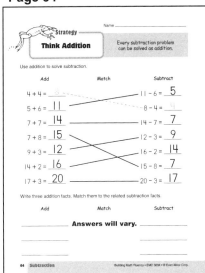

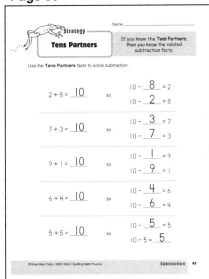

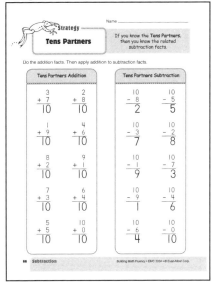

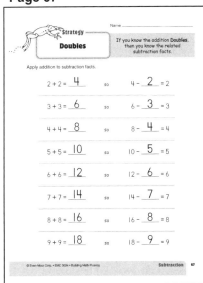

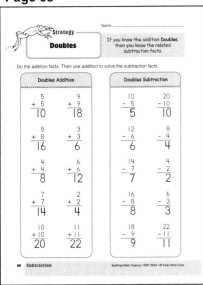

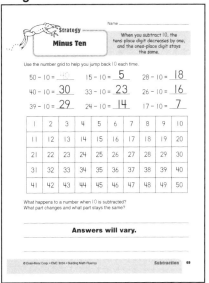

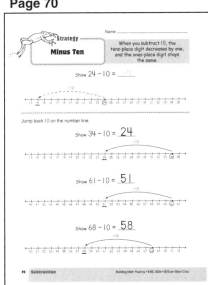

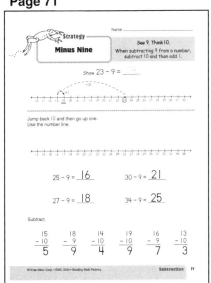

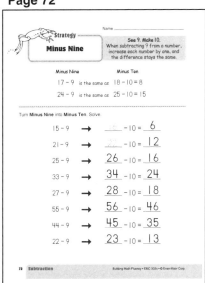

Page 73

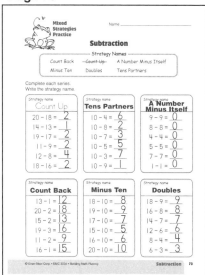

Mixed Strategies Practice

Name _____

Subtraction

Strategy Names
Count Back · Count Up · A Number Minus Itself
Minus Ten · Doubles · Tens Partners

Complete each series.
Write the strategy name.

Strategy name Count Up	Strategy name Tens Partners	Strategy name A Number Minus Itself
20 − 18 = 2	10 − 4 = 6	9 − 9 = 0
14 − 13 = 1	10 − 8 = 2	8 − 8 = 0
19 − 17 = 2	10 − 7 = 3	4 − 4 = 0
11 − 9 = 2	10 − 5 = 5	5 − 5 = 0
12 − 8 = 4	10 − 3 = 7	7 − 7 = 0
18 − 16 = 2	10 − 9 = 1	1 − 1 = 0

Strategy name Count Back	Strategy name Minus Ten	Strategy name Doubles
13 − 1 = 12	18 − 10 = 8	18 − 9 = 9
20 − 2 = 18	19 − 10 = 9	16 − 8 = 8
15 − 2 = 13	17 − 10 = 7	14 − 7 = 7
19 − 3 = 16	15 − 10 = 5	12 − 6 = 6
11 − 2 = 9	16 − 10 = 6	8 − 4 = 4
16 − 1 = 15	20 − 10 = 10	6 − 3 = 3

Page 74

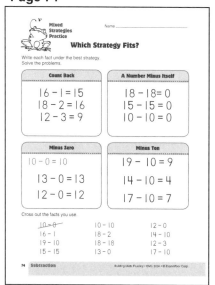

Mixed Strategies Practice

Name _____

Which Strategy Fits?

Write each fact under the best strategy.
Solve the problems.

Count Back	A Number Minus Itself
16 − 1 = 15	18 − 18 = 0
18 − 2 = 16	15 − 15 = 0
12 − 3 = 9	10 − 10 = 0

Minus Zero	Minus Ten
10 − 0 = 10	19 − 10 = 9
13 − 0 = 13	14 − 10 = 4
12 − 0 = 12	17 − 10 = 7

Cross out the facts you use.

10 − 0	10 − 10	12 − 0
16 − 1	18 − 2	14 − 10
19 − 10	18 − 18	13 − 0
15 − 15	13 − 0	17 − 10

Page 75

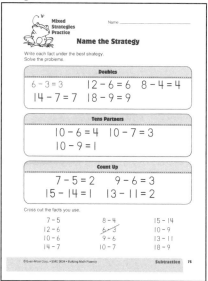

Mixed Strategies Practice

Name _____

Name the Strategy

Write each fact under the best strategy.
Solve the problems.

Doubles		
6 − 3 = 3	12 − 6 = 6	8 − 4 = 4
14 − 7 = 7	18 − 9 = 9	

Tens Partners		
10 − 6 = 4	10 − 7 = 3	
10 − 9 = 1		

Count Up		
7 − 5 = 2	9 − 6 = 3	
15 − 14 = 1	13 − 11 = 2	

Cross out the facts you use.

7 − 5	8 − 4	15 − 14
12 − 6	6 − 3	10 − 9
10 − 6	9 − 6	13 − 11
14 − 7	10 − 7	18 − 9

Page 76

Mixed Strategies Practice

Name _____

Subtraction Challenge

Subtract.

19 − 3 = b 16	3 − 3 = y 0	19 − 8 = r 11	17 − 9 = y 8	17 − 1 = b 16
20 − 5 = g 15	9 − 5 = y 4	6 − 5 = y 1	12 − 6 = g 6	20 − 6 = y 14
18 − 9 = r 9	16 − 8 = y 8	20 − 7 = b 13	6 − 0 = y 6	16 − 7 = r 9
17 − 6 = r 11	14 − 8 = y 6	18 − 5 = b 13	11 − 5 = y 6	17 − 8 = r 9
13 − 1 = g 12	12 − 7 = y 5	13 − 12 = y 1	7 − 1 = y 6	16 − 4 = g 12
23 − 20 = y 3	11 − 9 = y 2	16 − 6 = r 10	11 − 8 = y 3	18 − 2 = b 16

If the difference is between	Color the square
0 and 8	yellow
9 and 11	red
12 and 15	green
16 and 20	blue

Page 80

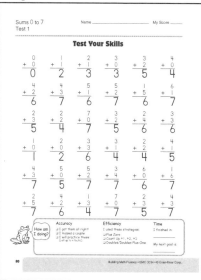

Sums 0 to 7
Test 1

Name _____   My Score _____

Test Your Skills

0 +0 0	1 +1 2	2 +1 3	3 +0 3	3 +2 5	4 +0 4
4 +2 6	4 +3 7	4 +1 5	5 +2 7	1 +5 6	6 +0 6
2 +3 5	3 +1 4	7 +0 7	3 +2 5	0 +6 6	2 +3 5
1 +1 2	1 +2 3	2 +6 ...	...	...	...

(Addition facts with sums 0 to 7)

How am I doing?

Accuracy — I got them all right! / I missed a couple / I will practice these
Efficiency — I used these strategies: Plus Zero / Count Up +1, +2, +3 / Doubles/Doubles Plus One
Time — I finished in ____   My next goal is ____

Page 81

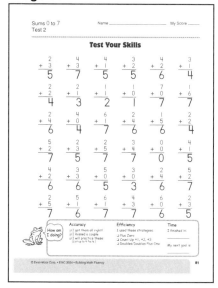

Sums 0 to 7
Test 2

Name _____   My Score _____

Test Your Skills

(Addition facts with sums 0 to 7)

How am I doing?

Accuracy — I got them all right! / I missed a couple / I will practice these
Efficiency — I used these strategies: Plus Zero / Count Up +1, +2, +3 / Doubles/Doubles Plus One
Time — I finished in ____   My next goal is ____

Page 82

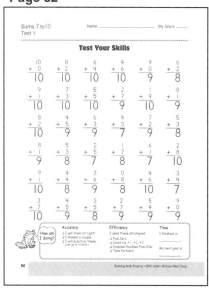

Sums 7 to 10
Test 1

Name _____   My Score _____

Test Your Skills

(Addition facts with sums 7 to 10)

How am I doing?

Accuracy — I got them all right! / I missed a couple / I will practice these
Efficiency — I used these strategies: Plus Zero / Count Up +1, +2, +3 / Doubles/Doubles Plus One
Time — I finished in ____   My next goal is ____

Page 83

Sums 7 to 10
Test 2

Name _____   My Score _____

Test Your Skills

(Addition facts with sums 7 to 10)

How am I doing?

Accuracy — I got them all right! / I missed a couple / I will practice these
Efficiency — I used these strategies: Plus Zero / Count Up +1, +2, +3 / Doubles/Doubles Plus One / Tens Partners
Time — I finished in ____   My next goal is ____

Page 84

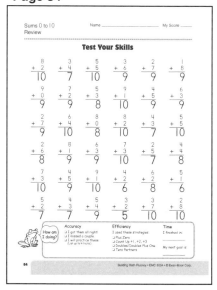

Sums 0 to 10
Review

Name _____   My Score _____

Test Your Skills

(Addition facts with sums 0 to 10)

How am I doing?

Accuracy — I got them all right! / I missed a couple / I will practice these
Efficiency — I used these strategies: Plus Zero / Count Up +1, +2, +3 / Doubles/Doubles Plus One / Tens Partners
Time — I finished in ____   My next goal is ____

Page 85

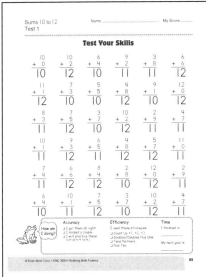

Page 86

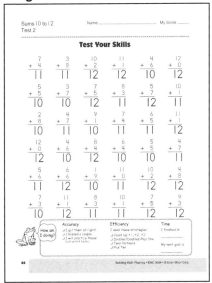

Page 87

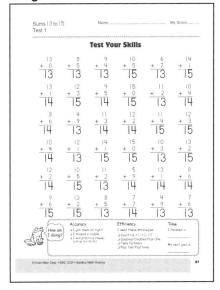

Page 88

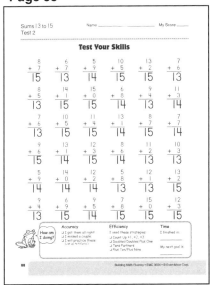

Page 89

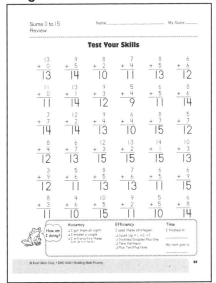

Page 90

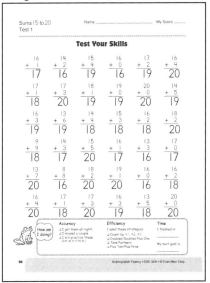

Page 91

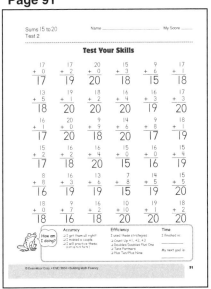

Page 92

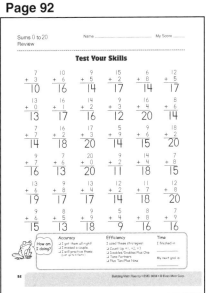

Page 93

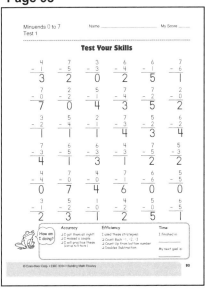

Page 94

Page 95

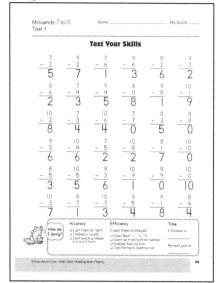

Page 96

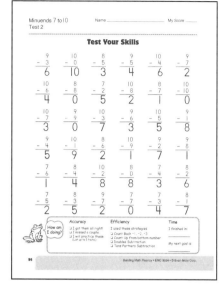

Page 97

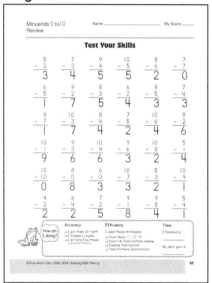

Page 98

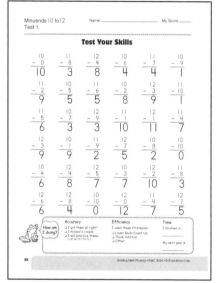

Page 99

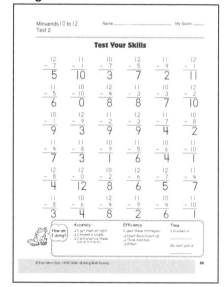

Page 100

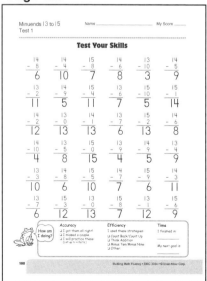

Page 101

Page 102

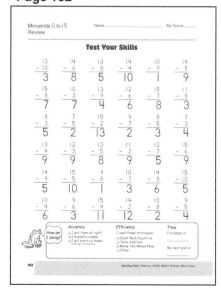

Page 103

Page 104

Page 105

Page 106

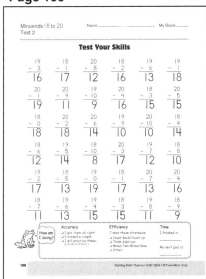

Page 107

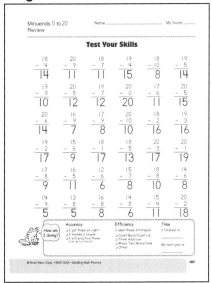